Part of My World

Part of My World

What I've Learned from *The Little Mermaid* about Love, Faith, and Finding My Voice

Jodi Benson

WITH CAROL TRAVER

TYNDALE
MOMENTUM®

A Tyndale nonfiction imprint

Visit Tyndale online at tyndale.com.

Visit Tyndale Momentum online at tyndalemomentum.com.

Tyndale, Tyndale's quill logo, *Tyndale Momentum*, and the Tyndale Momentum logo are registered trademarks of Tyndale House Ministries. Tyndale Momentum is a nonfiction imprint of Tyndale House Publishers, Carol Stream, Illinois.

Designed by Dean H. Renninger

Unless otherwise indicated, all Scripture quotations are taken from the *Holy Bible*, New Living Translation, copyright © 1996, 2004, 2015 by Tyndale House Foundation. Used by permission of Tyndale House Publishers, Carol Stream, Illinois 60188. All rights reserved.

Scripture quotations marked MSG are taken from *The Message*, copyright © 1993, 2002, 2018 by Eugene H. Peterson. Used by permission of NavPress. All rights reserved. Represented by Tyndale House Publishers.

Scripture quotations marked NIV are taken from the Holy Bible, *New International Version,*® *NIV.*® Copyright © 1973, 1978, 1984, 2011 by Biblica, Inc.® Used by permission. All rights reserved worldwide.

For information about special discounts for bulk purchases, please contact Tyndale House Publishers at csresponse@tyndale.com, or call 1-855-277-9400.

Library of Congress Cataloging-in-Publication Data

A catalog record for this book is available from the Library of Congress.

ISBN 978-1-4964-5327-3

Printed in the United States of America

28	27	26	25	24	23	22
7	6	5	4	3	2	1

Dear God,

thank You for my blessed life

thank You for my forever love, my husband, Ray

thank You for our incredible children, McKinley & Delaney

thank You for my loving family & my compassionate friends

but most of all . . . thank You for Your everlasting love!

Contents

"Wait till You Meet Her!"
BY PAIGE O'HARA

Musical theatre can be a tough business. It's mostly rejection, and the successes are few and far between. If you don't have really good friends to lean on and help you get through the rough patches, it can be a real struggle. But sometimes God brings just the right person into your life, and when that happens, it feels almost magical.

Back in 1981, I was playing Ado Annie in a national touring production of *Oklahoma!* alongside a talented young performer named Ray Benson. Ray was a triple threat. He could sing, he could dance, and he could act. He was also funny, charming, and very good-looking, so naturally, every unattached girl in the cast was making a play for him. I was married, so I wasn't looking. As it turns out, neither was Ray. He was head over heels in love with a girl he'd just met doing summer stock in Nashville. It was a tale as old as time—boy meets girl, boy gets part in touring production of *Oklahoma!*, boy leaves girl behind but can't stop thinking about her. All throughout rehearsals, he kept going on and on about *Jodi*.

"Wait till you meet her, Paige," he kept telling me. "Just *wait* till you meet her."

A few weeks later, when we were performing in Toronto,

I finally got my chance. Jodi had come up for the weekend to see Ray on her way out to Los Angeles to start rehearsals for a Broadway revue. She was very pretty, very sweet, and initially very shy. But as soon as we started talking about singing and musical theatre, the floodgates opened, and we talked for hours.

We had a lot in common. We were both big belters by nature (think singing in a 2,500-seat auditorium without a mic). We were both working on developing our lyric soprano voices because the more vocal ranges and styles we could master, the more opportunities came our way. I had just started working with a voice coach, but Jodi could sing any style—operatic, jazz, folk, gospel, pop—and she could belt a C like nobody's business. She was incredibly talented and eager to learn everything she could about the business and about honing her craft. Where we really connected, though, was our faith.

I remember telling her, "Look, there are going to be long stretches of times when you're not working, and that can be really, *really* hard. You've got to be ready for that."

Jodi just smiled and said, "Well . . . I have a strong faith, so I think I'll be okay." As we continued to talk, it was clear that Jodi's faith meant everything to her, and that spoke volumes to me about her character. She had a quiet confidence about her, but she was also very humble. She didn't see her vocal ability as a talent but rather as a gift she had been given, and she felt responsible for developing it and using it well. She just had an amazing attitude.

By the time Jodi left that weekend, I was every bit as taken with her as Ray was. Forty years later, I'm still one of her biggest fans, and I consider myself blessed to count her as one of my dearest friends.

Needless to say, when Jodi was cast as Ariel, I was beyond excited for her. When I called to congratulate her, I told her, "This is going to change your whole life." Of course, Jodi being Jodi, she just kind of laughed it off like I was being silly. Between Howard Ashman, Alan Menken, Disney Animation, and Jodi, though, there was far too much talent involved in *The Little Mermaid* for it to be anything *other* than a phenomenal success.

The thing is, Jodi didn't just play Ariel; Jodi *is* Ariel. She has that same adorable innocence about her—wide-eyed, optimistic, bubbling with enthusiasm, always believing the best about everyone, and seeing everything in a positive light. She really does believe that if she works and dreams and fights hard enough, she can achieve whatever she wants. And her career bears that out. She's also one of the most loving, giving, and supportive people I've ever met.

When I was working with Howard Ashman during my audition process for *Beauty and the Beast*, he kept referencing Jodi's work on *Mermaid*, so I kept trying to make my voice go up higher, like Ariel. But Howard told me, "I don't want it higher. You've got Belle inside you. Just let her come through."

I was so frustrated. I wanted to get it right—not only to make Howard happy but also because I loved Belle—we were like kindred spirits. I was always the oddball growing up. I was a total bookworm, and I quit cheerleading in high school to do theatre. While all the cool kids were listening to Led Zeppelin and Three Dog Night, I was listening to George Gershwin and Judy Garland.

I just could *not* figure out what Howard wanted. So . . . I called Jodi. After all, who knew Howard Ashman better than she did?

"I don't know what to do," I told her. "When I listen to the playbacks, I just feel like I sound too mature or . . . *too old.*"

Jodi didn't even hesitate. She just jumped right in with words of encouragement.

"You've got to trust yourself, Paige. They want an old-soul quality, and you've got that. Stop trying to be someone else. Just be you, and you'll be fine." She also gave me a few helpful tips about working with Howard, which was incredibly gracious. That's the kind of person Jodi is.

And you know what? She was right. When I went back in and sang with my natural voice, Howard loved it.

I can't even begin to tell you how grateful I am that Jodi and I got to share that unique experience. We're the only two Disney princesses who got to work directly with Howard before we lost him, and that's such an incredible blessing.

Years later, Jodi and I got to share another distinct honor when we were both named Disney Legends. It was so much fun standing at the edge of the stage watching Ray and their kids beam with pride as Jodi received that honor.

Even more fun, Lea Salonga, who was the singing voice of Jasmine and Mulan; Anika Noni Rose, who voiced Tiana; and Linda Larkin, who was the speaking voice of Jasmine, were also honored that day, so Jodi, Lea, Anika, and I got to sing a medley together.

Now I should point out that our quartet wasn't part of the original plan, but when you've got Ariel, Jasmine, Mulan, Tiana, and Belle together in one room, how disappointing would it be if they *didn't* sing something? So I offhandedly suggested the idea to the folks at Disney, and they loved it! The next thing I knew, they had worked it into the program.

Here's the kicker: I have always struggled with horrible stage fright. And I mean *horrible*. I was usually okay once I actually started performing, but until that first note came out, I was a hot mess. Fortunately, one of the things I had always loved about performing with Jodi was that she would pray with me before we went on stage, and that always helped calm me down.

Anyway, we all got together to rehearse before the ceremony. Since Belle doesn't have a full song, I was going to sing a medley of "Belle," "Something There," "Beauty and the Beast," and "Be Our Guest." I made it through the opening part okay, but when I came to the final note of "Be Our Guest," which ends on an E, I had some trouble. Cue the nausea and flop sweat. I thought, *I can't do this.*

The next thing I knew, Jodi was walking across the stage. She leaned in and whispered, "Paige, sweetie, you're an amazing belter. Just take it down to a C." She had a point. I had been belting out Cs my entire career. Even when I'm nervous, it just comes naturally. All of a sudden my nerves settled, and I thought, *Yeah . . . I can do that.*

"Okay," I said. She gave me a quick hug and walked back off the stage. The last thing I heard before the piano picked back up was Jodi saying, "You've got this, Paige. Belt the C." And I did. It might not have been my greatest performance, but it was definitely one of my favorites.

I *still* love performing with Jodi. We don't get to do it as often as we used to, but stage fright or not, I will never pass up an opportunity to share the stage with her as she sings "Part of Your World." Even after all these years, her voice has not changed one bit. And neither has she. She's still the same happy-go-lucky, I-can-do-anything-I-set-my-mind-to

Jodi she was when we first met. Not that she hasn't had her share of heartaches or disappointments. No one is immune to those. But her faith has given her the ability to weather the storms and come out stronger on the other side.

In an industry where true lifelong friends can be hard to come by, Jodi has been one of the best, and it's been a privilege to follow along on her journey and get to know the woman behind the voice. There is so much more to Jodi than just *The Little Mermaid*, and I am so excited that people are finally going to get a chance to see that.

That lovestruck young guy from *Oklahoma!* was right. She really is something special.

Just wait till you meet her.

Paige O'Hara

A Quick Note from Jodi

Hello, sweet friend! Thank you so much for taking the time to read this book. I sincerely hope you enjoy it. But before you start, I have a quick confession to make: I never wanted to write a book. Never. As in "ever."

I realize this may sound strange coming from someone who has performed in front of people her entire life, but the truth is, I'm not very comfortable talking about myself—especially in this season of life. I'm much more comfortable being a cheerleader for others. So when Tyndale approached me about sharing my story, it was honestly the last thing I wanted to do. Not only was it completely out of my comfort zone, but given all the mistakes I've made in my life, I also thought, *Who am I to give advice?*

But as a Christian, I do believe in being obedient and in following God's call—even when I feel like He's asking me to do something really uncomfortable, like this. Don't get me wrong: I love, love, *love* sharing my faith with others. I've just never done it in writing before.

Add to that the fact that I suffer from what I call "BC (before children) brain," so a lot of what happened before 1999 is—admittedly—a little hazy. It's entirely possible

I may not have recalled everything correctly, and in some cases, I may have messed it up completely. I promise I did my best, though, so I am hoping you'll extend me a little grace.

I guess what I'm trying to say is . . . this hasn't been an easy process for me at all, and at times I've been very frustrated and have even cringed a little, wondering if I'm making it sound as though I have all the answers—because I definitely don't. The truth is, I've made more mistakes than I can count. But if by sharing some of them I can help someone get from point A to point C without having to suffer the pain and heartache of point B, then all of this will have been worth it.

Writing my story has also given me the opportunity to shine a much-deserved spotlight on some of the incredibly gifted people I have had the privilege of meeting and working with over the years. Many of them made it possible for me to even be on this journey, and that's another reason this whole thing will have been worth it.

Whatever you take away from this book, please know that the story you're about to read isn't mine; it's His. The path God has led me on has not always been easy, but I wouldn't trade it for a million anythings. Because the journey so far . . . has been kinda beautiful.

God bless,

Jodi

1

"Maybe He's Right"

Maybe there is something the matter with me.

Why can't I get this?

"Sorry." I shook my head in frustration and took off my headphones.

"It's okay, Jodi. You're doing great."

I looked over at the control room, smiled, and mouthed "Thank you" to John Musker, one of our brilliant directors. Enshrouded in shadows, he was flanked on the left by our other director, the equally gifted Ron Clements.

God bless those guys.

It had been a long, frustrating afternoon. We had already recorded multiple passes of "Part of Your World," and I *still* hadn't nailed it. It seemed everything I did was too big, too loud, or—my personal favorite—too "Ethel Merman-y." In other words, "too Broadway."

I felt terrible, but I just couldn't help it. Up until now, my entire career had been Broadway and stage work—eight shows a week. Belting my heart out in front of 1,500 people at the Lunt-Fontanne Theatre was all I knew. I'd never worked behind a studio mic before, and four hours and almost a dozen passes in, it showed.

Fortunately, John and Ron had been incredibly patient and supportive. Add in our composer, Alan Menken, and lead animator, Glen Keane, and I couldn't have asked for a better creative team. Each one of them truly was second to none. Well . . . maybe second to *one*—the "one" being the man standing just off to my left. The one staring at my sheet music with laser-like intensity: the captain of Team Ariel—Howard Ashman.

Howard was, in a word, brilliant, and his lyrics were absolutely amazing. The first time I heard him sing "Part of Your World" on a demo tape, it brought tears to my eyes. "Under the Sea" is simply phenomenal, and I would have given anything to have been a background singer on "Kiss the Girl"—maybe one of the frogs or a turtle—just to be a part of it. The harmonies, the rhythm—everything about that song is just incredible. The man was a genius. This movie was his heart and soul, and frankly, I felt like I was letting him down.

I looked over at Howard and, in an apologetic tone that had pretty much been my go-to since lunch, asked, "Am I still a little too loud?"

"No," he assured me, his eyes never leaving his lyrics. "You're great."

"It doesn't feel like it," I confessed.

"No, really," he insisted. "You're doing great. Just . . ." He closed his eyes and steepled his fingers together at the end of his nose in his trademark "Howard's about to have a break-through" posture.

Poor guy. I could practically hear the gears turning as he tried to come up with some way to keep me from bungling his beautiful lyrics. Because despite everything my wonderfully supportive team was saying, in my mind I wasn't doing too great.

Of course, if anyone could find a way to make this work, it was Howard. He was the ultimate perfectionist—a master of lyrical nuance—and he was always, *always* right. I trusted him completely. We all did.

When he finally opened his eyes and looked at me, I was ready. No matter what he asked, somehow I was going to make it happen.

"Stop singing."

Okay, maybe I wasn't ready.

"Sorry?" I asked.

"Don't sing. Don't perform. Just . . . talk to Flounder, like you're talking to me right now." He said it very matter-of-factly, as though it were the most obvious solution in the world. I just stared at him blankly.

"Your performance is fabulous, by the way," he quickly added.

Well, at least there's that.

"You're just oversinging it."

And then there's that.

"Don't think of it as a song," he explained. "Think of it as a monologue. It's Ariel's inner monologue spilling over. It just happens to be set to pitch."

A monologue set to pitch. I liked that. I liked that *a lot*, actually.

"Don't worry about singing every note perfectly," he continued. "It's not going to be a perfect pass."

Okay, that I *didn't* like as much. Howard wasn't the only perfectionist in the room. As a Broadway singer, I'd been trained to sing every note to its full value, with perfect diction and full vibrato. Trying to sing a song "not perfectly" went against everything I knew.

But Howard was on a roll. "Don't focus on the notes. Focus on the lyric. Focus on the story. Try to imagine what Ariel's feeling at that moment . . . how much she loves her collection and how *excited* she is to be showing it off to Flounder.

"'*Look at this stuff!*'" he whispered excitedly. "'*Isn't it neat?*' People have to *feel* what she's feeling. They have to believe it's real."

I tried my best to mimic what he had just done. "Look at this stuff! Isn't it neat?"

Still too loud, I corrected myself.

"Try using less voice," Howard suggested, "but more intensity."

"Less voice, more intensity," I echoed.

"Yeah."

"So even *less* singing . . ."

"Exactly," he said, nodding.

I don't know if I can do this. I took a deep breath. "Okay, I'll try."

I slipped my headphones back on and nodded toward the control room so they knew to cue up the guide track. As the opening melody started to play, I glanced back up at Howard, his face illuminated by the tiny lamp on my music stand. He smiled at me and whispered, "You've got this."

Stop singing. Don't focus on the notes. Just talk to Flounder.
I shook my head and stifled a laugh. *Maybe he's right.*

Of course he was right. When it came to interpreting lyrics, Howard was always right. Still, who would have thought the best musical advice I would ever receive would be "stop singing"? Actually, that afternoon in the studio, Howard keyed me in to a pretty radical truth—sometimes the real magic is in the flaws.

"Part of Your World" is a beautiful song, but it's not perfect—at least not the way we recorded it. In fact, if you listen to it carefully, you'll notice that a few notes are kind of pitchy. Some notes are a little too sharp; others are a little too flat. Sometimes there's vibrato; sometimes it's more breathy. And sometimes the words aren't so much sung as they are spoken. It's not a perfect pass, not by a long shot, and yet that's exactly what makes it work.

Sing it perfectly and you'll still have a beautiful song, but you'll lose what makes Ariel, Ariel. And I just love her! I love how she loves life. I love how she savors every moment and delights in every experience. I love the way she sees the beauty in even the most mundane things. I mean, honestly, who else could get *that* excited about a fork? I love the way she holds nothing back, is open to everything, and believes the best about everyone.

All the passes we recorded that afternoon weren't so much about capturing Ariel's voice as they were about capturing her heart, and I couldn't have done it without Howard. Virtually everything about the way I portrayed Ariel came from him. I may have provided the vocals, but he provided everything else. I just did everything exactly the way he did it.

That doesn't mean it was easy. In fact, I'm sure somewhere

deep within the Disney archives there are miles of tape of Howard teaching me not to sing. And yet when all was said and done, somewhere between "Look at this stuff" and "Someday I'll be . . . ," a little mermaid found her voice, and a belter from Broadway learned that it's okay to surrender a few notes in order to tell an authentic story.

I owe so much to the fiery little redhead I got to know in the recording studio that day. She's given me an amazing career, an incredibly fulfilling ministry, and the opportunity to share my faith with thousands of people the world over. The privilege of providing Ariel's voice truly has been a gift from God. Any one of a million other girls could have done it, and it certainly wasn't the career path I was heading down at the time. But God knew exactly what He was doing when He started me on this extraordinary journey. I just had to trust and follow Him.

The best part? We don't have to be perfect. Because you know what? Life isn't a perfect pass either. We're going to make mistakes. I know I have. But I like to think I've learned a little something from each of them. And though some were incredibly painful, I also like to think they've made me a better person, a better wife, a better mom, and a better friend.

Nobody's perfect. The goal is to keep trying, to keep learning, and to keep trusting God. Looking back, I can see His fingerprints all over my life—in the doors He's opened, in the ones He's slammed shut, and in all the extraordinary people He's placed in my path at just the right moment and for just the right reason. He knew every mistake I was going to make before I made it, and He was always there to pick me up and steer me in the right direction when I went off course. It wasn't always the direction I'd *planned* on going, but it was always the right one.

God may have given me the gift of music, but He never asked that my voice always be perfect. All He has ever asked is that I listen, do my best, and go wherever *His* voice leads. That's all He asks of any of us.

2

"I Want More"

When you pursue a career in musical theatre, there are certain things you just come to accept: rejection, financial uncertainty, the insane amount of time spent filling out unemployment forms, and of course, the remote yet surprisingly real possibility that your entire career might someday hinge on the attention span of a restless preschooler. Trust me—it can happen.

Before *The Little Mermaid* officially released, the powers that be decided to hold a series of special screenings to gauge audience reaction to a rough cut of the film, and because it was a kids' film, one of these screenings was made up almost entirely of small children. As the film played, the execs in attendance weren't just watching the movie—they were also watching how the kids watched the movie. Where did their attention lag? Which lines and characters got the biggest laughs? The kids' reactions would help them decide what cuts or changes needed to be made before the animators put the finishing touches on everything and the movie was released into the world.

As chance would have it, about 15 minutes into the film, just about the time Ariel was pondering how many treasures one cavern could hold, a little boy dropped his bucket of popcorn. It's okay. Kids drop things. No big deal. Unfortunately, he happened to be sitting directly in front of then chairman of Walt Disney Studios, Jeffrey Katzenberg. Even more unfortunate, given the choice of listening to me sing or cleaning up the mess he had just made . . . you guessed it: That little guy got down on the floor and started scooping his popcorn back into the bucket. Now as much as I would love to give him the benefit of the doubt, as the mother of two, I can assure you, the average preschooler is *not* that fastidious. Clearly, we had lost the kid. Well, that's all Jeffrey needed to see. Convinced "Part of Your World" was too long and boring to hold kids' attention, he told John and Ron right after the screening, "You know, I really think we need to cut that song."

Cut "Part of Your World."

From *The Little Mermaid*.

Let that sink in for a minute.

Hard to imagine, isn't it? It's like trying to picture *The Wizard of Oz* without "Over the Rainbow." In fact, that's the exact argument that Ron and John made to Jeffrey, because believe it or not, *that* song was almost cut too—and for the same reason: *Kids won't get it.* But can you honestly imagine *The Wizard of Oz* without it?

Of course, Ron and John had both worked in animation

a lot longer than Jeffrey, and they knew these movies needed to appeal to audiences of *all* ages. The goal was to have the whole family there—Mom, Dad, Grandma, Grandpa—so there had to be something in the film to appeal to each generation.

"You're going to have a couple of minutes here and there when the little ones are going to get restless," they argued. "That's normal." But to lose that song . . .

Howard, of course, was furious. After all, an awful lot was riding on those lyrics. We had only three minutes and thirteen seconds to convey all of Ariel's pent-up teenage angst, confusion, and longing. Three minutes and thirteen seconds to make people understand why she is so willing to defy her father, enter into a deal with Ursula, leave everything she knows behind, and risk possibly never seeing her family again. Just three minutes and thirteen seconds to get a theatre full of people to identify with her, fall in love with her, and root like crazy for her to get what she wants. If you take that song away, you lose all of that.

Howard once explained it to me this way: "Part of Your World" is what people in musical theatre call an "I want" song, and pretty much every musical has one. It usually hits early on—maybe two or three numbers in—when the leading lady sits down or wanders center stage and sings about her hopes and dreams. In *Little Shop of Horrors*, for instance, Audrey sits on a garbage can and sings about moving off skid row to "Somewhere That's Green." In *My Fair Lady*, a shivering Eliza Doolittle sings "Wouldn't It Be Loverly?" to get "far away from the cold night air,"[1] and of course, little orphan Annie sings that haunting lullaby about "Maybe" someday finding her forever parents. Once the audience knows what their heroine wants, they spend the rest of the show *wanting* to see her get it. Having come from Broadway, Howard knew how important Ariel's "I want" song was to the rest of the film. Jeffrey, on the other hand, still needed some convincing.

In the end, it was animator extraordinaire Glen Keane who saved the day. You see, the thing about rough cuts is, they're rough. They're usually not fully colorized yet, and they don't always have all the fun little details that really make a scene pop. Back when animated features, including *Mermaid*, were drawn completely by hand, the animators didn't bother with the finishing touches until they were sure the scene was going to stick. While that saved the studio a lot of time and money, unfortunately it meant that the advance screening didn't always contain the most visually appealing footage.

Somehow Glen convinced Jeffrey to let him finish animating the scene to make it more vibrant and appealing to kids. Jeffrey agreed, Glen cleaned up the animation, and the next test audience *loved* it! The song not only stayed in the film but also went on to become one of the most beloved and iconic ballads in Disney history. Clearly, some things were just meant to be.

To this day, Jeffrey fully acknowledges that cutting "Part of Your World" would have been one of the biggest mistakes of his career. And thank goodness he didn't, because to be perfectly honest, I'm not even sure where I'd be right now if he had. Those three minutes and thirteen seconds literally defined my career and changed my life forever.

In addition to being Ariel's signature song, it's also become mine. I've sung "Part of Your World" at least once a week for more than 30 years now. It's a staple at every concert and event I do. I've sung it at wedding receptions, birthdays, anniversaries, and memorial services, and do you know what? I never get tired of it. Nor do I ever get tired of seeing the joy that song brings to people. It's just so relatable. I mean, who at some point hasn't dreamed of breaking away from their humdrum existence to experience something new and exciting?

I sometimes call it "The Big Reach"—the dream that is so huge, it seems almost unattainable. You don't even want to talk about this desire because once you put it out there, other people will be watching to see if it actually happens. And you know what? It might not. And that's okay. It doesn't mean you should stop dreaming, lower the bar, give up, or be more realistic.

Dreams aren't supposed to be practical or logical. They might not even make sense. Dreams are our hearts' desire. They have to be bigger than what we believe is attainable. That's what makes them dreams. All we can do is give each one over to God, pray about it, and trust that if it's part of His plan, it'll happen. And if it doesn't, it probably means He's got something even better in store for us.

Look at me. I didn't set out to do voice-over work. I just loved singing and wanted to see if I could make a decent living at it. I had my sights set on Broadway, but God took that dream and made it into something even bigger and better than I ever imagined. That's one of the great things about God: Whatever we want . . . He always wants more.

3

"What Good Is Sitting Alone in Your Room?"

Like Ariel, I was also the youngest of a musical family. My parents, Audrae and Harry, both had beautiful voices; my brother, Jeff, sang and played in a garage band; and my sister, Jill, sang and played the guitar. (And yes—we were Jeff, Jill, and Jodi—our parents actually did that.)

According to my mom, my musical career started when I was still in my high chair, and by the time I was six, it was all they could do to get me to stop singing. Then when I was nine, Jill taught me how to play the guitar on a little six-string my parents had given me for Christmas. She was an alto and I was a mezzo-soprano, so we created wonderful harmonies together. Once I mastered the basic chords, we started playing the guitar Mass at church on Sundays and even sang together at a couple of weddings.

Sadly, when I was 11, my parents divorced, and Mom and I moved out of our house and into a little apartment in our hometown of Rockford, Illinois. Jeff and Jill were older and living on their own by then. Thank goodness for Nana (my mom's mom). She was a godsend to me during that difficult season—always there to listen and provide encouragement and support. I honestly don't know what either my mom or I would have done without her.

Still, it was a hard, lonely time. After school, I would usually go straight to my room, close the door, lay all my music books out on the bed, grab my guitar, and sing my heart out for hours. I don't know what it was about singing; there was just something about it that gave me an overwhelming sense of peace. Everything else would magically fall away, and it was just me and the music.

I had dozens of songbooks—music by Cat Stevens, Carole King, Joni Mitchell, James Taylor, and of course, my favorite—Barbra Streisand. I think I owned every piece of music she ever performed. I especially loved "Evergreen." In fact, I think I performed that song at almost every wedding I sang at during high school. I also loved "People" and "The Way We Were," but who are we kidding? There's no such thing as a bad Streisand song.

I would listen to her recordings over and over, and then try to imitate them. I've always had a knack for picking up different dialects and the way different singers breathe, pronounce words, and turn a phrase. No matter the artist, whatever the song, I could listen and then sing it exactly the way I'd heard it—kind of like a mockingbird.

Joni Mitchell and James Taylor are both very folksy, which makes them a lot of fun to sing along with, but Streisand is extremely difficult to imitate. She has such an extraordinary range and tone, and she can shift between her chest voice and her head voice so effortlessly. She also has the most amazing breath control of anyone I've ever heard. If you listen closely (which I did), you can hear her take a quick catch breath here and there, but her ability to carry over phrases is so incredible, I swear sometimes it sounds as though she has sung an entire verse all in one breath. Back then I just loved what she could do with her instrument, and I still do. I couldn't approach her breath control or ability (who can?), but I loved the challenge of trying to mimic her, and I would spend hours giving it my best shot.

I was involved in every production during high school as well as in our local community theatre. I was even fortunate enough to play Maria in *West Side Story* one summer. I absolutely loved being onstage and performing. Something about it just felt right to me—not so much the applause, but the experience of losing myself in a song. I still love that feeling.

So when it came time to start thinking about college, I zeroed in on schools with strong musical theatre programs. I desperately wanted to go to the University of Cincinnati College-Conservatory of Music (CCM), which is ranked as one of the top programs for the performance arts, but finances were really tight, so I had to stay in state. Fortunately, Millikin University, located in central Illinois, had just launched a BFA in musical theatre. It might not have been the Conservatory, but they had dance studios, vocal studios, multiple theatres, and a full complement of acting, dance, voice, opera, and theatre courses. Plus it was a really tiny campus—only 1,200 students—which I loved. The only downside was that it was a private school, so it was a little pricier than some of the state schools in Illinois, but I figured if I could get a partial scholarship, it just might be doable. All I had to do was nail the audition.

There was just one small problem. The week before my audition, I came down with a full-blown case of the chicken pox. I was literally covered from head to toe with blisters. Even worse, my illness had started to spread to my throat and lungs. In fact, my doctor was concerned that if we couldn't get it under control, I might have to be hospital-ized. Fortunately, it didn't come to that, but I was still bat-tling a high fever, a miserable sore throat, and an allover inflamed, oozing, incredibly painful rash. Thank God for oatmeal baths—and Mom.

Mom had always been incredibly supportive of my inter-est in musical theatre, and along with my sister, Jill, she was my biggest cheerleader. She still is. Granted, I don't think she ever really expected me to make a career out of it, and deep down, I think part of her was hoping I'd settle on a more practical, "bankable" degree.

Even *I* had a fallback plan. I planned to major in pre-law while taking as many music and theatre courses as I could. I wasn't particularly interested in the law itself, but the thought of standing up in front of a packed courtroom pleading a case seemed at least vaguely theatrical. I figured by the time I finished my general-ed coursework, I'd have enough theatre classes under my belt to know whether I had what it took to make a go of it professionally, and I hoped against all hope that I did, because that was all I really wanted to do. And there was no way I was going to let a poorly timed case of the chicken pox stand in my way.

So when the big day arrived, Mom coated me in

calamine lotion, helped my fever-ravaged body into the car, and drove me four and a half hours downstate to Decatur, Illinois, "the Soybean Capital of the World." Not exactly Broadway, but a girl's gotta start somewhere.

It was a long drive to begin with—nothing but sweet corn and soybean fields for miles. Add in a fever and a couple of dozen festering scabs, and you, my friend, have got yourself one horrific road trip.

"Are you sure you don't want me to call and see if they can reschedule you?" Mom asked (multiple times).

"I'll be fine," I assured her. Granted, that might have sounded slightly more credible had I not been clawing at my legs like a lunatic as I said it. "They have to make their final decisions by the end of this month. If I don't do it now, that's it. I'm out." So . . . yep, no pressure there.

By the time we got to campus, my fever had broken slightly, but I was still feeling pretty wiped out, and my choice of audition material probably wasn't going to help. I had decided to sing "Cabaret" and had even worked out some choreography to go with it. I wasn't overly concerned about the vocals—provided my voice held out. I had listened to Liza Minnelli's rendition so many times, I had it down pat. But the thought of pulling those black fishnet stockings over my scab-encrusted legs and squeezing into that long-sleeve leotard made my skin crawl. Suffice it to say, that afternoon my life was anything *but* a cabaret.

It took me a sweet forever to get dressed. On the upside, the long sleeves and stockings did a pretty good job of hiding the scabs, and I was able to cover the ones on my face with stage makeup. I definitely did not look my best, but I figured that with the right lighting . . . and provided that the evaluators were sitting far enough away, there was a *slight* chance I could pull this off.

The auditions were held in one of the smaller theatres on campus, and thankfully the judges' table was set back so they wouldn't be able to get too good of a look at me. I just had to get through the entire performance without passing out or losing what was left of my voice.

When they called my name, I made my way to the center of the stage. Five evaluators sat side by side behind a long table out in the audience, each brandishing a freshly sharpened pencil, ready to critique my every note and move.

I rarely get nervous when I perform, but this was a really big deal for me, and I felt horrible. Plus, thanks to the fever, I was starting to sweat—and itch.

"Whenever you're ready, Ms. Marzorati," the man at the far end of the table called out.

"Yes, sir." I smiled and nodded for them to cue up my music.

Please, God, let me sound better than I look.

I honestly don't remember anything after "What good is sitting alone in your room?"[1] Based on the compliments I received afterward, I assumed my voice must have held up. And of course, I was still standing. Given the circumstances, I honestly couldn't have asked for much more.

A few weeks later, I received a letter telling me I had been awarded a scholarship that would cover just under half a year's tuition and room and board—the biggest one they offered. I was officially on my way!

I really do believe that when God gives you a gift, He's going to give you a way to use it—not just for your own enjoyment, but to bless others as well. There's a great verse in the Gospel of Matthew that says, "No one lights a lamp and then puts it under a basket. Instead, a lamp is placed on a stand, where it gives light to everyone in the house."[2] For whatever reason, God blessed me with the gift of song. That's my light. And as much joy as I got singing just for myself growing up, the only way for me to truly honor that gift was to develop it to the best of my ability and try to find some way to use it to bring that same joy to others.

I had no idea where that audition was going to lead. And I certainly never imagined it would take me where it did. I just knew this was something I loved doing, so I took a leap of faith and gave it my best shot. God did all the rest. And all the rest . . . *that* has been the greatest gift of all.

4

"What I Want from You Is . . . Your Voice"

"I really don't think I can sing higher than a C."

Steve just looked at me and smiled. "Yes, you can."

God bless Steve Fiol. He was my vocal coach my first year at Millikin, and he was amazing.

I had always been a big belter. In fact, a lot of Broadway singers are belters, which is basically the same vocal register you use to shout. I had always assumed that was all I could do. And then I met Steve.

We started off with some simple warm-ups. He had me sing through the scales using different vowel and consonant sounds—*mi mi mi; ma ma ma; mo mo mo*—that kind of stuff, going from low to high and then back down again. He kept pushing me to go higher and higher until finally I completely ran out of breath and all that came out was a little squeak.

"Told ya," I said, laughing.

"Yeah . . . you're not quite there yet." He chuckled. "But trust me. I was at your audition. You can belt, but you also have another whole part of your voice you're not even using."

I was skeptical.

"You're your own worst enemy," he used to tell me, and he was right. Singing is, by its nature, very emotional, which means a lot of your performance is internal. Once you have it in your mind that you can't do something, it's over. You've got to believe in yourself, and that kind of faith can't come from someone else; it has to come from you. Now obviously, it helps immensely when you have a coach who's kind, encouraging, and always saying, "Come on, you've got this!" But you really do need to have it inside you because that person isn't always going to be around. I got there eventually, but I was so grateful that I had Steve that first year.

Over the next several weeks, he walked me through a series of physical exercises and visualization techniques to help me "unlock" my voice. Some days he would have me sing entire songs while I was bent completely over at the waist with my head between my knees. Other times he'd have me sing while marching around the room, knees high, swinging my arms up and down like a drum majorette. I know it sounds a little crazy, but a lot of numbers in musical theatre require you to sing and dance simultaneously, so you've got to have plenty of stamina and solid breath control. You can't afford to get winded in the middle of a song. Steve also had me hang halfway out the classroom window and sing at the top of my lungs. "Let it go, Jodi!" he'd say. "Let it go!" I felt a little ridiculous, especially when other students would walk by and stare, but he was right—it *was* strangely freeing.

He also taught me some techniques to lessen the strain on my vocal cords so they wouldn't become fatigued as quickly. I had no idea how much tension I carried in my neck and jaw when I sang. It wasn't a nervous kind of tension; I just had a tendency to tighten up, stand really straight, and push my chin out when I sang, which meant that my breath was coming from the upper part of my chest as opposed to my diaphragm, where you want it to come from.

I also had to learn *how* to listen to myself, not just in a "You can do this!" sort of way, but literally. When you listen to yourself sing, you're not hearing what other people hear. It's kind of like when you hear your own voice on a recording or in a video. It doesn't sound like you—at least not the way *you* hear yourself. And believe me, in music, that can be a *huge* hurdle to overcome.

I can't tell you how many times I'd stop in the middle of a lesson and say, "Oh gosh. That was terrible," only to have Steve say, "No! That was it. That was perfect!" I'd be like, "Really? Because it sure didn't sound perfect." He constantly had to remind me not to trust what I was hearing in my head.

"Trust what *I'm* telling you," he'd say. And eventually I did.

That was one of the things I loved most about Steve. I didn't have to worry about making mistakes in front of him. Our lessons were all about experimenting and taking risks. Yeah, I messed up a lot, but that was the whole idea. That's how you grow. Whenever I hit an off note or something didn't come out quite the way we expected it to, Steve would just wave it off. We'd have a good laugh over it, he'd make a couple of suggestions, and we'd try it again.

And again.

And again.

Vocal cords are just like any other muscle. You have to train them, and that takes time and practice. Even the most gifted athletes can't run a marathon right off the bat. They start small and work up to it. It's the same with singing. And every once in a while, you have to push yourself beyond what you *think* you're capable of to see what you really *are* capable of. I was extremely fortunate that Steve created a wonderfully safe and encouraging environment for me to take chances in.

For example, one afternoon I walked into our weekly lesson, and he handed me some sheet music. I looked down at the music, then back up at him. "This isn't in English."

"Nope," he said, taking his seat behind the piano. "It's Italian. It's from Puccini's *Gianni Schicchi.*"

I raised my eyebrows. "Opera?"

"Yep."

"But . . . I can't sing opera."

"Sure you can," he said. God bless Steve. I knew he loved opera and taught classes on it, but at the risk of pointing out the obvious . . .

"I don't know how to speak Italian."

"You don't have to," he said with a shrug. "It's all phonetics. I'll teach you."

I just stared at him. "You're serious."

"Yep." He smiled.

I looked back down at the sheet music and tried to make sense of the lyrics. That's when I noticed that some of the notes were at the high end of the lyric soprano range.

"These notes are *really* high," I said.

"Yes, they are."

We had been working on my upper register for a while,

and I was doing pretty well. But this was coloratura, which was a different animal altogether. Unlike lyric soprano, which is what you typically hear in musical theatre, coloratura is more operatic and involves a lot of fancy runs and trills—all in the upper register. That meant I was going to have to sing not only higher but also with a much richer, fuller sound.

"You've got the range, Jodi," Steve assured me. "You're already a first-class belter. If you can add lyric soprano and coloratura to your résumé, you could be a triple threat."

I hated to admit it, but he was right. Most musicals typically have a lyric soprano who plays the romantic lead and a belter who's usually more of a comic relief. In *Oklahoma!*, for example, you have Laurey (the lyric soprano) and Ado Annie (the belter). Most singers are either one or the other, but not many cross over. And typically, singers who can do coloratura—and do it well—are almost exclusively operatic. If I could pull off all three, I'd have a much easier time getting work.

"Okay," I said with a shrug. "Let's give it a try."

We worked on that song for several weeks. I had a general idea of what I was singing about, and I was able to make sense of a few of the words, but for the most part I focused on mastering the technique—enunciating every syllable properly, projecting, managing the vibrato, and making sure I hit every last note to its fullest value.

By the time Christmas break rolled around, I could barely read my sheet music through all the notes I had made, but I had done it! I'd sung that entire aria—in Italian, trills and all.

By the end of spring semester, I was singing pieces in

French and German. That's what a phenomenal vocal coach can do.

Honestly, I think that sometimes we all need someone who believes in us more than we do—someone who will give us that little extra nudge of support and encouragement when we feel like we've reached our limit. I know I do, especially when I get locked into one of those negative thought patterns where all I can hear is *I can't.* Thankfully that's when God usually sends just the right person to help me see all the potential I *do* have, if only I'm willing to try.

I've been fortunate enough to have a lot of those people in my life. Some, like my mom and my sister, have been there from the very beginning. In fact, Jill continues to be my best friend and confidant and a model of unconditional love. When I was 12, I gained an amazing stepbrother, Allan. He and his wonderful wife, Kathy, have been by my side, cheering me on every step of the way. And Liz, my big sister in my sorority, was a constant support during my time at Millikin and has become a lifelong friend. Others, like Steve and Howard, were only in my life for a season. But that doesn't mean their impact or influence was any less important or appreciated.

Years after those sessions with Steve, I sang with my daughter, Delaney, who was in high school at the time, for a fundraising event. We sang the duet "For Good" from the musical *Wicked.* There is such a wonderful lyric in that song:

> *People come into our lives for a reason*
> *Bringing something we must learn*
> *And we are led*
> *To those who help us most to grow*[1]

I really do believe that's true. I think God constantly steers people onto our paths to provide much-needed encouragement, to shepherd us through the difficult times, and to help us reach our full potential.

Even now, I am incredibly blessed to have a wonderfully intimate network of family and friends whom I can turn to when I'm not sure what to do or when I feel like I'm in over my head.

Of course, the voice I listen for more than any other is God's. He knows me better than anyone—what I'm capable of, where I excel, and where I tend to fall (or sell myself) short—and He has my best interest at heart. His voice is *always* there, guiding and encouraging me, even when my cheerleaders are not around. That's the voice from within— that voice inside that tells me, *Don't be afraid, for I am with you. Don't be discouraged, for I am your God. I will strengthen you and help you.*[2]

That quiet voice has guided me throughout my entire career, and it's still guiding me today in every decision I make and in everything I do. And just as with Steve, I don't have to worry about making mistakes in front of Him. God knows that I'm not perfect and that I need help. That's *why* He's always putting people like Steve and Howard in my path. God's just got a knack for knowing which people will bring out the best in each other. Speaking of which . . .

5

~~~~~~

"I Saw You and the World Went Away"

In January of my freshman year, a notice went up on campus about open auditions at the University of Illinois in Champaign for summer theatre jobs. People would be coming from all over the Midwest and parts of the South to audition. I felt I had grown a lot as a performer during my first semester. The question was, had I grown enough to sing professionally?

There was only one way to find out, so I made the 45-minute trek to U of I to audition. Dozens of places were looking for performers—mostly vacation resorts and community summer theatres. One, in particular, caught my eye—the Opryland theme park in Nashville. They were auditioning singers and dancers for a Broadway musical revue called *I Hear America Singing*, a decades show that covered the music of the twenties through the late seventies.

I figured, *What's the worst that can happen?* If I got a part, great. If I didn't, well . . . there were a lot of other places on the list. I'd just keep trying until I got a yes. Fortunately I had a really solid (and chicken pox–free) audition, and before I knew it, I had officially landed my first professional job.

As soon as the semester ended in May, I headed down to Nashville, found a cute (and cheap) little apartment with a friend from high school who was performing in another show, and started rehearsals. The sweetest husband-and-wife team, Bob and Jean Whittaker, were directing. Bob handled the music, and Jean was the choreographer.

God bless Jean. She was so peppy, so bright, so encouraging, and so, *so* pregnant. She had to be at least seven, if not eight, months along. Frankly, it was amazing how much she was still able to do. But when one of the cast members showed up four days late, Jean needed someone to help her get him up to speed. As it turned out, that someone was me.

"Ray," Jean began the introductions, "this is Jodi Marzorati. Jodi, this is Ray Benson."

I'm not gonna lie. The guy was gorgeous.

"Hi, Jodi." He stuck his hand out. "It's nice to meet you."

"Nice to meet you too." I smiled politely and shook his hand, suddenly aware that my heart was beating at roughly the same speed as a hummingbird's.

He looked to be in his early twenties, and he was a good four inches taller than I was with a square chin, chiseled jaw, and the most beautiful blue eyes I'd ever seen. When our eyes met, his mouth curved into a smile, and I felt my cheeks go red. Flustered, I promptly looked away and pretended to brush an imaginary strand of hair out of my eyes. *Smooth.*

Jean explained that Ray had just finished performing in a production of *West Side Story* in Birmingham, which is why he was joining us a little late.

I glanced back up at Ray and made a quick attempt to recover. "Shark or Jet?"

"Actually, I was playing Tony."

Wow. Gorgeous and talented.

"You seem surprised," he said playfully.

"No, I just . . ." *Shoot.* "Actually," I said, recovering, "I did a production of *West Side Story* last summer."

"You did?" He raised his eyebrows.

"Now who seems surprised?" I teased. *Two can play at this game.*

"Not at all," he replied, backpedaling. "Professional?"

"Community theatre." *That's still respectable*, I reassured myself. "Right after I graduated."

"Oh, cool. Where'd you go to college?"

"It was high school," I admitted sheepishly. *And now he thinks I'm 12.*

Jean mercifully broke back in. "Ray, Jodi's fantastic. She'll help you get caught up on everything you've missed."

"That'd be great." He smiled down at me appreciatively, and I felt my cheeks flush again. *What is wrong with me?*

"Jodi," Jean said, turning to me, "do you think you can get Ray up to speed by Monday?"

"Mm-hmm." I nodded. I had no idea what day it was.

Ray caught my eye again and smiled. Cue the hummingbird.

Oh yeah . . . I was in trouble.

As it turns out, Ray was an amazing dancer. I had to show him a routine only once, and he just naturally got it. The Charleston, swing, jazz, tap—Ray made it all look effortless. In just two nights, he had pretty much mastered what it had taken the rest of us almost a week to perfect, and frankly, it was starting to get on my nerves. I was trying so hard to get on equal footing with him after that whole flustered school-girl thing when we first met, but he wasn't making it easy. Neither was the fact that after two solid hours of dancing the Lindy Hop and jitterbug, he was barely even winded, while I was sweating like a horse.

And I wasn't the only one vying for his attention. I swear Ray caught the eye of every single girl in that cast. He had such a quick wit, and he was always joking around—doing silly voices and telling funny stories. Everyone loved hanging out with him—especially the girls. I suddenly wished I'd dated more in high school. I'd had a couple of minor "relationships" here and there, but nothing big or serious. And to be honest, flirting had never been my strong suit, which became more and more obvious every time Ray and I were together. I kept trying to play it cool and aloof, but somehow it just came off as bossy, which he teased me about constantly. Bottom line, I had absolutely no idea what I was doing, and to Ray's obvious amusement, it showed big-time.

Once our cast had the ensemble numbers down, it was time to audition for the solos and duets. By this time, Ray was in lockstep with the rest of the cast, but for the life of me, I could not get a read on him. I couldn't tell whether our constant sparring was masking some kind of spark, or if he was just tolerating me like he would an annoying kid sister. I needed some kind of sign. Then, out of nowhere, Leonard Bernstein showed up.

We all gathered onstage, and Bob held up two sets of sheet music from *West Side Story*. He asked for volunteers to sing "Tonight," the love ballad between Tony and Maria.

I looked directly at Ray. I couldn't imagine he wouldn't at least audition. Sure enough . . .

"I might as well give it a shot," he said, reaching for the music.

Then Bob turned to the girls. "Okay, I need a Maria."

"I'll do it," I said, raising my hand. He handed me the music, and Ray and I approached the piano. Ray had his usual confident smile, and for once, I had one to match. Ray knew I'd been in *West Side Story*. He did not, however, know I had played Maria. Neither did anyone else.

As the pianist keyed up the intro, I took a quick glance down at the music, but I didn't need it. I knew "Tonight" like the back of my hand. And of course, so did Ray.

Here's the thing. Once you've actually performed a song, it's *really* hard to sing it straight, without all the emotion, the gestures, and the choreography, so by the time I was four lines into it, Ray knew full well that I'd done this before. The look on his face was priceless. It had taken me almost a week, but I had finally done it. For once, Ray was the one who was speechless.

And then suddenly, he wasn't.

It was the first time I had ever heard him sing. He had the most beautiful tenor voice—deep, rich, full . . . perfect. Then, just as we reached the first chorus, Ray smiled, winked at me, and threw his music to the floor. Without even thinking, I threw mine down as well. Then he reached over, took both of my hands in his, and pulled me in close, and we went into full-on Broadway mode.

> *Tonight, tonight,*
> *It all began tonight,*
> *I saw you and the world went away.*[1]

The only thing missing was a mysterious spotlight appearing out of nowhere and a 30-piece orchestra swelling in the background. When we finally finished, the entire cast burst into raucous applause, and Ray and I collapsed into each other's arms, laughing.

"Okay then," Bob joked, "assuming nobody wants to try to follow *that* . . . I think it's safe to say *West Side Story* is cast."

The next few weeks were a blur. It was a grueling schedule. We did four to five shows a day, six days a week, to a packed house. I'd love to say it was solely because of our stellar cast and brilliant performances, but the fact that we were in one of the only air-conditioned venues at the park during the peak of the summer heat *might* have played a small role as well.

Actually, we *did* have a pretty stellar cast, and in spite of the ridiculous amount of time we spent together, we all got along beautifully. As for Ray and me—even though we openly declared our love for one another roughly 30 times a week in song, I *still* couldn't get a clear read on how he really felt about me.

Then a couple of weeks into the summer, a group of us decided to go to the movies on our night off. I was really looking forward to it, if for no other reason than to give myself a much-needed night off from hyperanalyzing every interaction Ray and I had during the day.

I showed up at the theatre a little early and waited out front for the rest of the group. After about 15 minutes, I bought my ticket and went inside to wait in the lobby. Ten minutes later, I was still the only one there. *Do I have the right show?* Then just as I was getting ready to leave, Ray walked in.

"Hey," he said, waving. Then he looked around. "Where is everybody?"

"Beats me." I shrugged.

"Huh." Ray looked at his watch. "They must be running late."

"Everyone?" I asked.

"Looks like it," he said, glancing around the virtually empty lobby.

"Maybe we've got the wrong theatre," I suggested.

"I don't think so." He checked his watch again. "Well, the movie starts in like five minutes. If they don't hurry up . . ."

By this point, even the kid behind the concession counter had figured it out. We'd been set up.

"Ray." I glanced up at him. "I don't think they're coming."

"I think you may be right." We stared at each other awkwardly for a few seconds; then Ray checked his watch one final time and sighed. "Well . . ."

Oh great, I thought. *He's probably gonna leave.*

But he didn't. Instead, he smiled, held out his hand, and asked, "Shall we?"

I couldn't tell you what we saw that night if my life depended on it—*The Blues Brothers, The Blue Lagoon*—I have absolutely no recollection. What happened next, however, is indelibly seared in my memory.

Ray walked me back to my apartment, and to his credit (and my disappointment), he was a perfect gentleman.

"This one's mine," I said, stopping in front of my door.

He glanced around the complex. "Looks nice."

"Yeah . . . it's okay." *Should I invite him in? No. Well . . . ? Wait . . .* I really was horrible at this.

"Well . . . thanks, Jodi. That was fun."

"Yeah . . ." *Say something.*

"So I guess I'll see you tomorrow then." He took a small step back.

He's leaving.

"Umm . . . Ray?" He took another small step back and I started to panic. Three weeks, almost 100 performances, and an obviously staged blind date—how many more chances was I going to get? So with all the subtlety of a freight train, I grabbed him by the shoulders, spun him around, shoved him up against the wall, and planted one on him.

Actually, now feels like a good time to mention that I'm really not that aggressive. But with every unattached girl in our cast ogling Ray on a daily basis, I figured that if I didn't put it out there first, someone else would. Still, it's not exactly the dewy, romantic first-kiss story I'd hoped to tell our kids someday: "Yeah, Mom basically threw Dad up against a wall."

Oddly enough, my first kiss hadn't been that much different. It was the end of eighth grade. I was at a graduation party for one of my friends, and a bunch of us were just hanging out and dancing to records. Someone put a slow song on, and a boy came over and asked me to dance. So we were bobbing back and forth, and out of nowhere, he leaned in and kissed me right on the lips. And it wasn't a clean kiss either. It was wet and sloppy, and even worse, it happened in front of everybody. He was a really sweet guy—I cannot overemphasize that enough—but he just wasn't anyone I had ever thought about in that way, and frankly, it caught me completely off guard. So I pushed him off, smiled politely, and said, "No, thank you."

Seriously—who says that? I was mortified.

Fortunately for me, Ray's kiss wasn't like that. In fact, it was quite the opposite. And it launched a romance that lasted throughout our time at Opryland. But like most summer romances, it was fleeting. A few months later, the show wrapped, and I had to go back to school. Ray was going to stay in Nashville for a few more months to do some television work, so we planned to take turns making the seven-hour drive between Decatur and Nashville so we could spend more time together on weekends.

When Mom came down to help me pack up my apartment and move all my stuff back to Millikin, we had "the talk." She had come down a few times over the summer to visit and see the show, so she had met Ray, and she really liked him. In fact, several of my family members had met him, and they all agreed he was a great guy. At the time, everyone—myself included—considered it a summer romance and nothing more. But now . . .

"So how do you feel about him?" she asked.

"I think I'm in love." There. It was out there. "And he said he loves me."

Granted, I was 18, and I'm not sure you really know at that age what love means, but Ray just seemed to check all the boxes. He was charming, funny, talented, handsome, and so, so kind. He genuinely cared about everyone in the cast and crew and had so much integrity.

Maybe it was because he was four years older, but he seemed so much more mature and responsible than any of the other guys I'd dated before. He was also incredibly driven and self-sufficient. He was not only supporting himself but also helping his parents financially.

Honestly, what wasn't to love?

"In fact," I said, figuring I might as well put it all out there, "I think I just met the guy I'm going to marry."

To Mom's credit, she was extremely supportive.

"Oh, that's wonderful, sweetheart."

She was also realistic.

"Why don't you just take it one step at a time and see what happens."

I think she figured, *She's 18, he's in Nashville, she's in Illinois . . . What could possibly come of this?* (Spoiler alert: We have two kids.)

But you know what? Sometimes when you know . . . you know. I mean, what are the odds that a girl from Rockford, Illinois, and a guy from Birmingham, Alabama, would both end up performing at the same theme park in Nashville? Or that Ray would show up four days late, and I would be assigned the task of getting him up to speed on the ensemble routines? Or that we would both have performed the respective leads in *West Side Story*? I sometimes wonder if certain things are just meant to be.

Of course, my family's approval mattered a great deal to me. If they hadn't liked Ray, that probably would have given me a pretty big check in my spirit about him. That's why I always run big decisions past a handful of people I trust before diving in headfirst.

Depending on the situation, I have a few people, like my mom and my sister, whom I know I can reach out to for advice about my career, my marriage, my kids—you know, the big stuff. They genuinely want the best for me, so I know they're not just going to tell me what I want to hear.

That day in the car, Mom told me not only what I *wanted* to hear but also what I *needed* to hear. "I'm happy for you. But let's take things one step at a time."

So that was the plan. I wasn't going to do anything crazy. I went back to Millikin, and Ray and I arranged our schedules so we could see each other as often as possible. We even found a way to split Christmas vacation between his family and mine, and over break, we auditioned for another summer revue called *Follies on Broadway*. It was similar to our Opryland show, only this time the tour would start in Los Angeles and then travel to Bermuda—not bad work if we could get it.

By the time I got back to school in January, everything was going beautifully: I loved my classes. I was a straight-A student. And I was waiting to hear back about a job that would allow Ray and me to spend a wonderful sun-kissed summer together performing in Bermuda.

Then I went and did something crazy.

6

"Sick of Swimmin', Ready to Stand"

"Remember when I told you that Barry Moss came out to see that production of *West Side Story* I did in Birmingham?" I could hear the excitement in Ray's voice over the phone.

Barry Moss was one of the top casting directors on Broadway, with a ton of connections in theatre, film, and television. He not only had seen Ray in *West Side Story* but had also been so impressed with his performance that he'd given Ray his card and told him to give him a call if he was ever looking for work. I can't speak for today, but back then, that kind of thing rarely happened.

"Yeah?" I replied.

"He got me an audition for the national tour of *Oklahoma!*"

"Wow. That's great! When is it?"

"I already did it."

"And?"

"I leave for Toronto in two days!"

"You got it? That's fantastic!" *Two days* . . .

I barely had time to process it before Ray broke in again. "That's not all. It's an Equity tour."

Wow. That was huge. Getting your AEA (Actors' Equity Association) card meant better pay, better hours, health benefits, a pension plan, first crack at exclusive auditions, and *hordes* of professional contacts.

I really was genuinely thrilled for Ray, but *two days* . . . I wouldn't even be able to see him again before he left.

"How long's the tour?" I asked.

"Seven months."

Seven months. There goes our summer together in Bermuda. Even if we *did* get cast, there was no way Ray would turn down an Equity tour for a nonunion summer resort gig. Nobody would. My head started swimming. *When are we ever gonna see each other?* I hadn't really thought about it before, but now that it was staring me in the face, I couldn't help but wonder, *How in the world do theatre couples make this work?*

Two days later, Ray headed off to Toronto, and I resigned myself to spending a long, lonely semester in central Illinois. I'm not going to lie; it was rough. I loved my classes, and I knew I still had a lot to learn, but now that I'd had a taste of performing professionally, it was all I wanted to do. I loved being onstage—the camaraderie with the rest of the cast, the lights, the makeup, the costumes, that rush of adrenaline that would kick in five minutes before the curtain went up and wouldn't fade until hours after the show had ended. I just loved all of it.

I also loved Ray. At least I was pretty sure I did. We called each other at least once or twice a week while he was in Toronto, but I found even that difficult. As much as I loved hearing about his work, attempting to make sophomore-level acting classes sound comparable to the thrill of doing live professional performances was virtually impossible. We were living in two different worlds, and that worried me. Everything was going well between us, and I knew Ray really cared about me, but for some reason I couldn't shake the feeling that it could all fall apart at any minute.

~~~~~~~~

One night toward the end of March, I was in my room studying when one of my sorority sisters stuck her head in the doorway.

"Hey, Jodi. Call for you. Some guy."

Probably Ray. I closed my book, threw on a pair of flip-flops, and headed down to the phone at the end of the hall.

"Hey, sweetie," I said, settling in against the wall.

"I'm sorry . . . ," a confused male voice responded. "I'm looking for Jodi Marzorati?"

Uh-oh. That's not Ray. I pushed myself back up, and in the most professional voice I could muster, I said, "This is Jodi Marzorati."

The company manager for the Broadway revue Ray and I had auditioned for at Christmas introduced himself.

"You auditioned for us a few months ago, and I'm calling to make you an offer."

Yes! "Oh, that's great! Thank you!"

"I'm also calling because we have a bit of a problem. Our leading lady broke her ankle during rehearsal yesterday, and we'd like you to take her spot."

Leading lady? My heart practically leapt out of my chest.

"I'd need you to be in Los Angeles in about three weeks."

Then my heart dropped into my stomach.

What do I do? On the one hand, I couldn't think of anything I'd *rather* do. But I had another month and a half of classes, plus finals, and I was in the middle of a show on campus.

My mind started spinning. *What would happen if I just skipped the rest of the semester? What would Mom say? Would she be upset? She might be. Then again, she knows how much this means to me. I'm sure Ray would tell me to take it. I'd be in Bermuda all summer. There's no way we'd be able to see each other. Of course, we probably wouldn't be able to see each other anyway. Maybe Millikin would let me move my finals up a few weeks. It's only half a semester—not even . . .*

"Are you still there?"

"Sorry," I quickly apologized. "Yeah, I'm still here."

"Well, what do you think? By the way, I should mention that the contract would run through the end of October."

Well, there goes fall semester. Shoot. I didn't know what to do.

Then he mentioned the salary. It would more than cover the rest of my tuition—through graduation. *There's no way Mom would argue with that. Plus Ray just got his Equity card. I'm already so far behind him . . .*

Why was I even arguing with myself?

"Yes. I'll be there."

The next morning, I made the rounds to all my professors to explain the situation and see if there was any way I could salvage that semester's work. I started with Steve.

"Oh, you've got to do it, Jodi," he said. "It's what you're training for. The experience alone will be priceless."

I'm not going to lie, that helped—*a lot.* So did the fact

that the rest of my profs said basically the same thing. Not only that; they also agreed to let me move my finals up so I could get full course credit, which, in addition to the salary, helped Mom get on board as well. Ray, of course, was totally supportive. In fact, pretty much everyone was in agreement that this was a fantastic opportunity and that I'd be a fool *not* to take it.

Everyone except one.

The dean of the fine arts program was dead set against it. He said I wasn't ready yet—that I needed more training and that there would be plenty of time to do professional shows later. I should finish my degree first, he insisted.

I have to admit, that did give me some pause. But I just kept hearing Steve and Ray and all the others in my head saying, *Go for it*. Six months in Bermuda, almost all expenses paid, enough money in the bank to pay for the rest of college with a little left over, and a leading role in a professional production to add to my résumé? Steve was right. This *was* what I was training for. So why wait?

Sometimes you've just got to take a leap of faith.

Granted, I did value my professors' opinions. If all of them had strongly advised against it, I *might* have reconsidered. Wait—who am I kidding? No, I wouldn't have. That's what a leap of faith is—a willingness to trust in something you can't actually see or prove.

That professional experience was going to benefit me a lot more than formal training in the long run. And it's not as though the doors at Millikin were going to be closed to me forever. I could always go back to school the following spring, but there was no guarantee I'd ever get another opportunity like this.

Frankly, if either of my kids were to come to me with a similar situation tomorrow, I'd tell them, "Go! Give it your best shot! See what happens. If it doesn't work out, that just means God has something even better in store for you. And no matter what happens, Dad and I will always be here, and we will always love and believe in you."

The people I trusted the most believed in me, and sometimes that's all it takes. That, and a little bit of faith.

7

"Ask 'Em My Questions and Get Some Answers"

Setting aside the fact that I had just "unofficially" dropped out of school, I was a pretty responsible kid. I had a great work ethic. When I was young, my dad owned a laundromat, and by the time I was 10, I was working there every Saturday, using a toothbrush to clean the dried-up detergent and grit out of the edges of the top loader doors. I know— gross, right? But Mom always used to say to me, "Would you want to pull your nice clean clothes out of a filthy washing machine?" Well . . . no. In fact, to this day, I still wipe down my machine at home between almost every wash.

And I never got into trouble at school. I didn't dare. I went to a Catholic school, and most of the teachers were either priests or nuns, so we pretty much stayed in line. Once when I was in first grade, I was caught talking in class. The teacher sent me to the principal's office, and as a punishment, I was locked in a closet with the lights off. It couldn't have been more than 15 minutes, but it was still pretty upsetting. I was crying, pounding on the door, and begging to be let out. And if you think *I* was upset, you should've seen my parents. They went straight to the school and let them know, in no uncertain terms, that this type of punishment was *totally* unacceptable. I don't know who was more traumatized by the whole thing—me, them, or my parents—but it never happened again.

Weirdly, a year or two later, I had a teacher who pulled down the shades on Friday afternoons, put on a 45 of "Venus," and let us dance on top of our desks. I have no idea how she got away with that. She wasn't a nun; I remember that much. But talk about a weird mix. One minute I was locked in a closet for talking in class, and the next minute someone was blaring rock and roll and inviting me to get up on my desk and dance. It's no wonder I had a lot of questions about God and religion growing up.

~~~~~~~~

Church was always a big thing in our family. We were there almost every Sunday, dressed to perfection—me with a veil on my head—and I loved it. I loved the music, the prayers, the fellowship, the stained glass windows depicting different scenes from Jesus' life, even the sacraments. Oh, I *loved* the sacraments, especially weekly confession. Don't ask me why. It's not as though I ever had anything of significance to confess. I remember sitting there in that little confessional box, racking my brain, trying to think of something to say, like *I was disrespectful to my mom, I didn't tell the complete truth,* or *I yelled at my friend and called her a name.* It was hard because it had to be legit. Still, there was something about getting down on that little kneeler that suddenly made it all so real and so personal. It wasn't just a ceremony or ritual. There was something going on there. I felt as though I were actually talking to God. The only piece I couldn't make sense of was why I needed to go into that little box and confess my sins to a priest. Why couldn't I just talk directly to Jesus?

I asked our priest that one day. He tried his best to explain it—something about the priest being "that step in between"—but it still didn't make sense to me. We used to pray at home before meals and at bedtime, and there was such a realness and authenticity to it. I didn't need anyone to stand in between me and Jesus then, so why should this be any different?

By the time I got to high school (also Catholic, by the way), I started to realize that Catholicism wasn't the *only* way to know Jesus. For starters, not everyone in our neighborhood went to St. James. Some of our neighbors were Lutheran, some were Presbyterian, and some were Pentecostal. I didn't fully grasp all the differences, and to a certain extent, I didn't really care. The only thing that mattered to me was my own relationship with God. I knew that was real, and it was a source of comfort when everything started falling apart at home. Though I rarely saw my dad after my parents' divorce, I felt peace knowing I wasn't alone since God was always with me.

~~~~~~~~~

Fast-forward to November '81. Ray and I had been together for almost a year and a half, and everything was going great.

He even flew out to surprise me one weekend while I was working in Bermuda. You don't get a lot of days off when you're on tour, and the fact that Ray used his to fly 2,000 miles just to see me for one day meant the world to me.

Then one day out of the blue, Ray called to tell me he had been doing a lot of soul-searching and had "recommitted himself to Christ." I'd known Ray was a person of faith when we started dating, and he knew that I was, too, but if I'm being honest, neither of us was really living that out. Now Ray told me he wanted us to have a more "God-centered" relationship. Frankly, I wasn't even sure what that meant, and it rattled me. Despite the physical distance between us, I felt like we'd grown closer as a couple. Now all of a sudden, Ray was talking about boundaries and wanting to slow things down. It just felt like a giant step backward.

Ray asked me to visit him in Los Angeles to talk more about it. He had been crashing at a friend's house there since the *Oklahoma!* tour ended, and he had become good friends with a local pastor and his wife. Apparently, they had helped him get back on track spiritually, and he was anxious for me to meet with them too.

Pastor Ed and his wife, Juanita, were the sweetest couple. Ray and I got together with them several times. I adored them both, especially Juanita. She was so incredibly kind and patient. She had to have known why Ray was bringing me around, but to her credit, she never pushed or pressured me. We would just sit in her kitchen and talk, sometimes for hours. Pretty much nothing was off-limits. We talked about my family, my parents' divorce, my childhood parish, school, work—but mostly we talked about Ray and me.

It was complicated.

The more Ray and I talked, the more obvious it became that something had changed in him spiritually, and I was getting the feeling that if I didn't resolve my own faith issues, we might not have a future together. Now, he never *said* that, but the subtext of all our conversations seemed to be, *This is the path I'm going down, and you need to make a decision for yourself.*

It wasn't as though I didn't believe. I prayed almost daily, so God was already part of my life. But what Ray, Pastor Ed, and Juanita were talking about was different. They were talking about a personal relationship, separate from church—a living, breathing, whole-life commitment—daily submitting every decision to Jesus and allowing Him to direct my every step.

I had to admit, it sounded both wonderful and overwhelming at the same time. I really liked what they were saying; I just didn't understand it. What did it mean to submit your life to Jesus? How did that work? What did it look like? And what if I couldn't figure it out? What would happen with Ray and me? Would that be it? Would it just be over?

I loved Ray, and I didn't want to lose him, but this was a *huge* decision. No matter what I decided, everything was going to change. I didn't know what to do.

Fortunately, Juanita did. One day she sat quietly and let me process all my fears and concerns out loud. When I finished, she smiled and said, "It sounds like you've got some pretty big questions."

And?

She leaned in and rested her hand on mine. "And that's great."

Is it? She seemed a lot more optimistic than I felt.

"It just feels like I'd be making a lot of major changes."

"But you wouldn't be," she quickly countered. "It's not about taking any one part of your life and drastically changing it. It's just adding on to what you already have. It's taking something you're already doing and making it more . . . *deliberate*. It's making God a part of *everything* you do, not just when you happen to think of it, but first and always."

Actually, that didn't sound anywhere near as difficult as I had imagined. In fact, it sounded pretty good. But I still couldn't picture what it would look like day to day, or with regard to my relationship with Ray.

Juanita must have known what I was thinking, because the very next thing she said was, "You just need to make sure you're doing this for yourself, no matter what happens with you and Ray. That can't be part of it."

I knew she was right. I had to take Ray out of the equation. *But how?* Ray was such an enormous part of my life. I wouldn't even have *had* this conversation if it hadn't been for him.

We talked a few more times, and I spent a lot of time thinking and praying on my own. I did take my faith seriously. God had always been such a grounding presence in my life, and the thought of making Him an even bigger part of it . . . well, that just sounded amazing. In fact, what they were describing sounded exactly like what I had wanted as a kid—to get rid of the middleman and talk to God directly—and not just in the confessional box or on Sundays, but whenever I wanted.

So the next time Pastor Ed, Juanita, Ray, and I got together, I told them, "I'm ready. I want to do this."

We went into the kitchen, and I sat at the table while they

all stood around me and rested their hands on my back and shoulders. Then Pastor Ed started to pray.

That's when it happened.

I started to shake, and I felt light-headed and nauseated.

"Are you okay, honey?" Juanita asked calmly.

"No." My voice was shaking almost as much as I was. "I think I'm gonna be sick." I started to panic. "What's happening?"

She stayed perfectly calm. They all did. "It's okay, honey. You've got a spiritual battle going on. Clearly, the enemy does not want you to make this decision."

What? I had heard about that kind of thing before, but . . . *Really? Me?* Suddenly, one dark, horrible thought after another started filling my head, making the nausea even worse. I was really starting to freak out, but Pastor Ed just reassured me. "It's okay, Jodi. You're fine. Those thoughts aren't really yours."

It was almost eerie how calm everyone was. I mean, I was a mess—shaking, coughing, crying. I hadn't seen any of that coming. But they were completely unfazed. Pastor Ed just kept praying.

"You have a choice to make, sweetie," Juanita said, her hands never leaving my back.

I took a deep breath and refocused. "Okay." Still shaking, I closed my eyes and said, "I am a child of God. I reject the enemy, and I accept Jesus into my heart."

As soon as I said it, I felt a major release. I stopped shaking, the nausea went away, and the horrible thoughts instantly disappeared. The whole thing couldn't have lasted more than a few minutes, but I felt as though I had just run a marathon. I turned around to face Juanita and collapsed into her arms, exhausted, but very much at peace.

To this day, whenever I start to question whether God really does have a calling on my life, I think back on that afternoon. I don't know how else to account for such a visceral reaction. I'm just grateful that I had such a kind and tender couple to help me through it. They listened to all my questions, they didn't judge, and they didn't push. They just helped me see what was right in front of me the entire time.

I still wasn't 100 percent sure what this new commitment was supposed to look like, or if I could do it. But I was 100 percent committed to trying.

Ray, of course, was thrilled. And while our new relationship looked a little different, it turned out I'd been wrong: We hadn't taken a giant step backward; we'd taken one forward. Praying together and knowing that our decisions came from the same moral and spiritual foundation made our relationship even stronger.

It also turned out that Juanita had been right. Even though my faith walk was very much entwined with Ray's, the commitment I made that day was genuine, and my faith was very much my own. And that was going to be important in the months ahead.

8

"Life's Full of Tough Choices, Isn't It?"

Remember when I said that I used to carry a lot of tension in my neck and jaw when I sang, and that I had to learn how to relax and let the notes come more naturally? Well, it turns out the same basic principle applies to love and relationships—at least it did for me.

After Ray and I got back from Los Angeles, we spent the holidays visiting with our families and reconnecting with each other after almost seven months apart. Everything was going beautifully. There was just one little hiccup—what to do next.

I'd had the time of my life performing in Bermuda. The experience was fantastic, and to be honest, I wasn't entirely sure I wanted it to end. Meanwhile, Ray had been talking with Barry Moss about going to New York in January to give

Broadway a shot. As it happens, he'd also been talking to Barry about me, and it was Barry's opinion that we should *both* come out to New York. The problem was, I was supposed to be going back to school.

As a certain sea witch once said, "Life's full of tough choices, isn't it?"

In Barry's mind, it was a no-brainer. "Work begets work," he told me. "You just finished a job. You're on a run. Why stop now? Keep going. Ride the wave."

And it wasn't just him. Steve, my mom, my sister, Ray—pretty much everybody I talked to thought I should go for it. I *had* saved almost every penny of what I'd earned in Bermuda, so financially speaking, I'd be okay for a while, even if I couldn't find work right away. It really seemed that God was opening the door. So when my stepbrother, Michael, offered to let Ray and me crash at his place in Manhattan until we could find places of our own, I decided to walk through it.

As soon as we arrived, Barry booked us auditions for the touring company of *Joseph and the Amazing Technicolor Dreamcoat*. We were both cast—Ray as Joseph's brother Judah and I as a member of the ensemble. I also got something else—my Equity card. *Joseph* wasn't just a national tour; it was a union tour as well. I had taken a chance and walked through one door. Now, thanks to Barry, there would likely be others. Even better, Ray and I were walking through this one together.

The tour hit all the major cities: Philadelphia, Chicago, Los Angeles, Miami, San Francisco, New Orleans, and Orlando. We stayed in each one for about a month, which gave Ray and me plenty of time to sightsee and explore. We both loved to hike, and we had a blast trekking around

Yosemite, Monterey, and Sequoia. It was wonderful getting to spend so much time together after spending almost a year apart. There was only one downside: We were spending *so much time together* after spending almost a year apart.

Ray was my first "serious" relationship, so I had no idea what I was doing, and I was battling *a lot* of insecurity.

While on the road.

For nine months.

With the guy I was pretty sure I wanted to marry.

And about 22 of our closest friends.

Eight of whom were women.

Cue the internal monologue: *Everything's fine. We're dating. Of course, we're not exclusive. Are we? Neither of us is seeing anybody else. At least I'm not. I'm sure he isn't. How could he? We're together all the time. Am I being too clingy? Should I give him some space? Maybe we should spend a couple of days apart. Hang out with other people. But what if he finds someone else? We* are *a couple. We should be spending time together. But is it too much time? I really should give him some space. Or maybe not. We* are *dating. I'm sure everything's fine. Isn't it?*

The fact that Ray wasn't super forthcoming with his emotions didn't help. So I played to my relational strengths—clingy and needy one minute, cool and aloof the next.

Yeah . . . I had everything under control.

After the tour ended, we went back to New York, where we each sublet an apartment from friends we'd made in the cast. Ten days later, Ray was cast in *Dreamgirls*. He would rehearse in New York for six weeks, then head off to LA. That's when he hit me with it.

"I don't think I love you anymore."

"What?"

"I just don't feel like we're the right ones for each other."

Where is this coming from?

"Is there someone else?" I literally held my breath.

"No, that's not it."

At least there was still hope.

"I just don't see anything long-term with us. I'm sorry."

And then there wasn't.

It's amazing how quickly things can go from great to terrible. Ray had brought so much joy, so much love, and so much laughter into my life. I couldn't imagine life without him. I was devastated—and if I'm being totally honest, a little hysterical.

I remember calling Juanita and just wailing on the phone. "How could he do this? Everything was going so well. I've done everything he's asked me to do, and now this . . . I'm gonna call him."

As she had done before, Juanita just listened quietly while I ranted and raved. Then after I had gotten it all out of my system, she calmly reminded me, "You're not a doormat, Jodi. If he wants some space to figure things out, you need to give it to him."

Easy for her to say.

"But he's gonna be leaving in a few weeks. What if—"

That's when *she* hit me with it.

"Sweetie, the best thing you can do right now is let him go. If God wants you two to be together, it'll happen. Remember, your step of faith was for you. It wasn't for Ray."

"Yeah, but—"

"Honey, Ray may not be the one that God wants you to marry."

Wow. I hadn't even considered that.

"You can't fight to keep him. You can't fight to win him back. You have no control over that."

"Well, what am I supposed to do?"

"All you can do is pray. You need to ask God to do one of two things—either increase Ray's love for you . . . or decrease your love for Ray."

So *that* was it. *That's* what giving my life over to God looked like—not rushing headlong into what *I* wanted but surrendering it to Him and listening for what He wanted.

So that's what I did. That's what I prayed for—daily. *God, if this is not what you want, then remove Ray from my heart. If it is, please help Ray to see it.*

Over the next several weeks, every time I was tempted to pick up the phone and call Ray, I called Juanita instead, and she would calmly and coolly talk me back down off the ledge. Then we would pray together. I'm not going to lie; it was hard. It was *so* hard—especially when Ray would call just to, as he put it, "check in and see how you're doing." Sometimes he'd leave me messages, asking me to call him back, but Juanita encouraged me not to reach out to him, to give him the space he needed. After all, she reminded me, that's what he'd asked for.

Life's full of tough choices. I had made mine. Now it was time for Ray to make his.

And then there was nothing.

Three months of radio silence.

No calls.

No messages.

Nothing.

Until . . .

"Why don't you come out to LA for a visit?"

God must have been doing *something* in my heart during those three long months because I immediately snapped back with, "Why would I do that?" (For the record, January Jodi would have been on the plane before he finished the sentence.)

"Well . . . because I miss you."

Huh. Maybe God was doing something in Ray's heart too.

As soon as we got off the phone, I called Juanita. "Should I do that?"

"Oh no, sweetie, you're not going to do that. You're not going to get on a plane and fly all the way across the country just because he says he misses you. He needs to figure out if he just misses being in a relationship or if he misses being in a relationship with *you*."

Again, easy for her to say.

And yet that's what I told Ray.

And then he went dark again.

As deafening as the silence was, it did give me a lot of time to think. I had spent the better part of a year and a half obsessing over every possible aspect of our relationship, trying so hard to control everything, and where had it gotten me? Sitting by myself in New York while Ray was off in LA doing his own thing. Maybe Juanita was right. Maybe Ray wasn't the guy I was supposed to marry.

The weird thing was, the more Juanita and I prayed about it, the more at peace I became with it. She was right. I couldn't control it. Ray had to sort his feelings out for himself and come to his own conclusions. The only way our relationship was going to work was if we were both equally committed to it. Otherwise, it wasn't a "committed" relationship. At least not the kind I wanted.

Speaking of which . . . Ray's radio silence also gave me the chance to reflect on the commitment I'd made that afternoon in Pastor Ed and Juanita's kitchen. As genuine as my decision had been, I *did* have an ulterior motive. Though I'm sure it wasn't his intent, I felt as though Ray had given me an ultimatum—either I got on board with him spiritually or we were finished. I had made the right decision; I'd just made it for the wrong reason.

God didn't just want me to say the words. He wanted me to mean them and to understand what they meant. I sometimes think that's why He let me go through the pain of that breakup—to bring me to a place where it was just Him and me, without Ray or anybody else muddying the waters. Just as Ray needed space to figure out how he felt about me, I needed space to figure out how I felt about God and what it meant to truly put Him first. I think God knew I wasn't spiritually mature enough to face these questions on my own. That's why He gave me Juanita—to help me through this time by holding me accountable and providing support until I was ready to stand on my own.

Three months later, Ray finally figured it out.

"I've been thinking a lot about what you said, Jodi, and I've been praying about it. And the thing is, it's not that I just miss being in a relationship; it's that I miss *you*. Would you *please* come out to Los Angeles so we can really talk?"

As excited as I was to see Ray again, something had shifted. I still loved Ray, and he was still incredibly important to me, but he was no longer *the* most important thing in my life. God had taken hold of my heart, and no matter what happened between me and Ray, I knew He was always going to be there and He would always come first.

A few weeks later, Ray and I were walking along the beach in Malibu when he asked me to marry him. He didn't have a ring. In fact, we were both in our bathing suits, so I'm not even sure he'd planned this proposal. It was Labor Day weekend, and Ray joked that he had been "laboring over this decision" for a while. He just needed some space to make sure it was right. We both did.

Of course I said yes. I didn't even have to think about it. As it turns out, not every choice is a tough one.

9

~~~~~~

"When's It My Turn?"

Let's talk about 1984 for a minute.

I was 22 and engaged to the man of my dreams, and I had just finished performing in my first Broadway show.

Wait . . . did I forget to mention that?

Whoops. My bad. It all happened so quickly. *Everything* in that time period happened quickly, except . . . well . . . I'll get to that.

Backing up a bit, about a month before I flew out to LA to see Ray, Barry Moss booked me an audition for the Broadway show *Marilyn: An American Fable*, which was based on the life of Marilyn Monroe. After two callbacks, they just knew. They had found their "ensemble factory girl."

Okay, so it wasn't a huge part, but I had done it! I had made it onto Broadway. Me, little Jodi Marzorati from Rockford, Illinois. It was literally a dream come true.

Here's where God stepped in. Normally we would have started rehearsals right away, but because it took them forever and a day to raise the funds and find a theatre, our start date kept getting pushed back, week after week after week, which is why I was *able* to go out to LA, which led to the talk, which led to the walk, which led to the proposal that Ray made.

The show was fraught with problems from the beginning. For one thing, there were 16 producers and 10 songwriters, none of whom could seem to agree on anything. We did 34 preview shows, during which the original director and choreographer, Kenny Ortega (who went on to have an absolutely brilliant career and is a fellow Disney Legend), was replaced; the role of Marilyn was recast; 10 different musical numbers were dropped; and almost an hour of dialogue was cut from the script. Sadly, I'm not sure any of it helped. We opened on November 20 and closed 14 days later in the wake of a scathing review from Frank Rich, the top theatre critic at the *New York Times*.

And that was it. My first Broadway show lasted exactly two weeks. But even though we did only 17 shows, it was a fantastic experience, and I had a great time doing it. How could I not? It was Broadway!

Anyway, flash forward through the holidays and, *bam*, it's 1984.

Ray and I got married in May at an adorable little church in Lake Geneva, Wisconsin, not far from where my mom and stepdad lived. And yes, Ray did eventually get me a ring. In fact, he proposed to me all over again at my parents' house over Christmas. As I recall, it was in the kitchen, and Ray's best friend from college, Jimmy, was there. Ray was nothing if not romantic.

Right after the wedding, we packed up Ray's '69 VW bus and drove back to New York. A few months earlier, we had bought a teeny tiny apartment in an old prewar building on 57th Street, between 9th and 10th Avenues. We got it at a steal as part of a fire sale, and never has a description been more appropriate. It was on the fourth floor, and its two little windows faced a brick wall. If you looked out and up, you could *almost* see a small patch of sky, but you really had to want it. And when I say teeny tiny, I mean teeny tiny. Wall to wall, it was a whopping 15 x 14, or about 210 square feet, the size of a decent master bedroom.

The kitchen . . . actually, now that I think about it, calling it a kitchen might be a little generous. The kitchenette included a little two-burner stove, a dorm-sized refrigerator, a tiny sink, and a couple of small cabinets hidden behind a set of old Pullman doors.

Thank goodness I had no idea how to cook.

Just to the left of the kitchenette was an even tinier bathroom. It was a little tight, but on those rare mornings when we both had to be out the door at the same time, Ray and I could fit in it together, as long as one of us didn't mind standing in the bathtub.

Ray moved in right after we bought it and started fixing it up so it would be ready when I got there, and to his credit, he made the most of every square inch. He even designed a custom loft-style bed that sat atop two chests of drawers to help make up for the lack of closet space, which allowed us to use our futon as a sofa. Ray also found a little pullout table we could use for meals and then slide out of the way to free up floor space so we could practice audition material. Our one luxury, aside from the microwave we got as a wedding gift, was a color TV Ray propped atop a four-drawer file cabinet that tripled as an entertainment center/nightstand/end table.

Our apartment might not have been much to look at, but the location was perfect—right in the heart of Hell's Kitchen, within easy walking and biking distance of the Broadway District.

The day we arrived, I sat on the floor, surrounded by all our stuff, and cried (poor Ray). Everything seemed to be happening so fast. One minute I was in college, going to classes and hanging out with my friends, and the next minute I was married and living in this little apartment, wondering where my next job was going to come from and how we were going to pay the bills.

Before, there had always been a fallback option. School had always been waiting in the wings, I had a room at my parents' house, and if Ray and I started to get on each other's nerves, we could retreat to our separate apartments for a little breathing room. But now my house literally *was* a room, my college days were seemingly over, and with only 210 square feet to play with, Ray and I couldn't get away from each other if we tried.

Fortunately, Ray and I weren't just married, we were also best friends, and we got along extremely well. Before long, we settled into a happy little routine, going to auditions and doing everything we could to keep our expenses down.

The fact that I could've burned water helped keep our grocery bills in check. Usually we'd just grab a quick sandwich at the deli around the corner or split a can of soup that Ray would heat up on the little two-burner. Then once a week, we'd splurge on a big night out—well, big for us. There was a great little Chinese place on 9th Avenue called

West Side Cottage. For 10 dollars, we could get an appetizer (we usually had the cold sesame noodles), an entrée (that we would split between the two of us), and two glasses of wine. We would catch the early bird special on Thursdays, many times with one of our dearest friends, Timmy, and then come home to our little apartment to watch *Family Ties* and *The Cosby Show*. Yep . . . we were livin' large. But we were happy. And that in itself was a big deal.

The entertainment industry can be so incredibly difficult. Nothing is guaranteed. You're never sure when your next job is going to come along or where it's going to be. Ray and I had already experienced both extremes—traveling together as part of the same show and being thousands of miles apart for months at a time—and frankly, both had their drawbacks. There's just a lot of stress no matter what.

One of you may be having a good day—nailing an audition or getting an offer—and the other may be having a bad day, sitting by the phone waiting for a callback that never comes. You genuinely *want* to be happy for each other, not only because you love one another, but also because it's a joint effort. You're both working toward the same goal and trying to survive. But there are a lot of stretches between shows when you're collecting unemployment and lying awake at night wondering when that next paycheck is coming.

And Broadway was different back then. The talent pool was a lot smaller and tighter, and you could move from show to show. But now the pool is huge, and you've got to compete with all the TV and movie stars making the jump from screen to stage. I can't imagine stepping into musical theatre work right now, and I have nothing but respect and admiration for those who are passionate enough and committed enough to give it a go.

Don't get me wrong: It's not impossible. Like any other industry, if you work hard, continue to hone your craft, and seize every opportunity as it comes, you *can* make it work.

Or if you're like I was, you can take an already difficult situation and make it even harder.

I mentioned that Ray and I continued to get a lot of auditions after we moved back to New York. What I didn't say was that I was turning a lot of them down.

I had already done a national tour and a Broadway show, and in both instances, I was part of the ensemble. Now, there was nothing wrong with that. Both parts were great, and both gave me great experience. But just as work begets work, in musical theatre a certain kind of work tends to beget more of the same kind of work. That meant I had a decision to make at this stage in my career.

I had just signed with Nancy Curtis, a phenomenal agent with Bret Adams, LTD, and an even more phenomenal person, and one of the first things she did was to sit me down and tell me just that. "If you want to pursue a principal role at some point, we need to start turning away ensemble opportunities," she said. "The longer you continue to do ensemble work, the harder it's going to be to make that transition. Now, if you're happy doing solely ensemble work, that's great. I just need to know."

The thing is, I wasn't. Some people love doing ensemble work. That's what they're created for, and they genuinely enjoy it. As much as I loved what I was doing, however, I wanted to tackle some roles with more responsibility. I didn't feel like I needed to have my name above the title or anything like that, but I also knew I didn't want to continue doing strictly ensemble parts.

"I'll do whatever you want, Jodi," Nancy told me. "I just need to know, because once you've drawn that line in the sand, there's no going back. So . . . what do you want to do?"

I wanted to talk to Ray. After all, my decisions didn't affect just me anymore. So one night, Ray and I sat down over a plate of cold sesame noodles and discussed it.

"What do *you* think?" he asked.

I hated it when he did that.

"I think I wanna go after principal roles. It's not so much a financial decision"—a bold statement as we sat there splitting a 10-dollar dinner for one—"but I'm 22 and trying to get myself established. I think Nancy's right. I need to draw a line in the sand and see what happens, even if that means I don't have anything going for a while. What do *you* think?"

He sat back in his chair and thought about it for a minute. "I think it's time. You need to do this. Don't worry about the money. We'll find a way to make it work. You go ahead and draw your line. Make the leap."

I *loved* it when he did that.

So I did. That's when 1984 came to a screeching halt.

Nancy started turning down auditions for roles in ensembles, and for the first time since my sophomore year at Millikin, I was unemployed.

For six months.

I realize that may not sound like a long time, but when everyone else around you is going to auditions, starting rehearsals, and getting ready to go out on tour, every week without a job offer can feel like a year.

I did have a handful of auditions, but principal roles were

fewer and farther between, and I was up against people with a lot more experience than I had. There were a couple of times I honestly thought I had nailed it. I not only felt great about my performance but also as if everyone in the room had felt it too—only to hear, "Thank you so much. We've decided to go another way." Some nights I just sat on our little futon and cried.

About four months and 14 early bird specials into the drought, I asked Ray, "Do you think I made a mistake?"

"What do you mean?"

"Well . . . I could probably audition for more shows right now if I just switched back to ensemble work."

I fully expected him to say, "If that's what you want to do. We could certainly use the money." But instead, he pulled a Ray and said, "Be patient, Jodi. God has more in store for you. I know He does. Just give it a little longer. Your time will come."

He was right. I was doing it again—trying to make things happen on my time instead of waiting on God's. A few weeks later, Nancy got me another audition, this time for one of the female leads in the touring company of *Sophisticated Ladies*, a revue featuring the music of Duke Ellington that had recently finished a successful two-and-a-half-year run on Broadway.

"Go in, enjoy yourself, and make the most of the moment," Ray told me. "And when you're done, just walk out and let it go. Remember, it's not in your control."

He was right—again. It wasn't in my control. All I could do was the best I could do, so that's exactly what I did. I went in, had a great time, enjoyed the audition . . . and that week, the sesame noodles were on me.

I finished out 1984 on the road. And would you believe it—one of the stops was a one-nighter at the Kirkland Fine Arts Center at Millikin University. It was as though God were saying, *See? I've got you. Just trust Me.*

And He does.

And I do.

Giving up control of your life is never easy. 1984 was like a master class in learning to surrender. I said goodbye to my home, my family, my privacy, my independence, and for a while, anyway, my earning potential. But the beauty of surrendering is that more often than not, you end up getting so much more than you gave up. I know I have.

Still not convinced?

Wait till you see what happened next.

10

~~~~~~

"Poor Unfortunate Soul"

Call me crazy, but I love the audition process. I genuinely enjoy the chance to try new things, meet new people, and make a few connections. If I happen to get the job—great! If I don't, well . . . that just means God has something else in store for me. Either way, I absolutely love it!

If you've never auditioned, here's basically how it works (at least how it *used* to work back in the day): When someone decides to put on a show, they hire a casting director, who sends out breakdowns of the principal (i.e., lead) parts to a select network of agents. *Your* agent then reads through the breakdowns, and if they feel like you might be a fit, they get you an audition. Typically auditions take place in five-minute time slots, and you juggle your schedule to accommodate whatever slot you can get.

On the day of your audition, you show up at the rehearsal hall, check in, and then take a seat and wait, usually in a long hallway alongside dozens of other people, many of whom look suspiciously like you.

Eventually they call your name, and you walk into a large room (most likely a dance studio) with mirrors along the walls and a long table set up in the back where the casting director, casting assistant, director, choreographer, composer, music director, stage manager, and—in some instances—the producer(s) sit. You say your hellos, hand them your headshot and résumé (which they probably already got from your agent, but you never want to show up without them), and then sing a 32-bar cut of a song—something that fits the style and range they're looking for and shows off your voice.

And that's it. You say thank you, head back home, and wait for the phone to ring. If they like you, they'll ask you to come back and read or sing—and sometimes dance—for a specific part before they make a final decision.

If they *know* you're not a fit for the part, they'll often call your agent at the end of the day and say, "Thank you so much, but we're going a different way." Getting those calls from your agent can be tough. In the beginning, every no is tough. After a while, though, you start to realize that those rejections have nothing to do with talent. After all, this is Broadway—you wouldn't be there if you didn't have talent. More than anything, the casting team is trying to find a specific look—a certain age range, body type, etc. They always send out principal breakdowns ahead of time, but they rarely get too specific, which is why I often found myself surrounded by dozens of other twentysomething, average-built, belting mezzo-sopranos who could dance.

Any time you hear no, you can't take it personally. You can't control the often highly specific image casting directors have in their heads of what a character should look or sound like or whether you would be a good visual match opposite whoever else they're thinking of casting. You've got to get yourself into that neutral headspace right away, or you're not going to make it. You'll drive yourself crazy about something over which you have absolutely no control. You can't let it get to you, because during the course of your career, there are going to be plenty of nos. But it takes only one yes to change your life.

Back in the mid-eighties, I was going to auditions left and right, and I heard "No, thank you" and "Sorry" much more than I care to mention, but by the time I made the switch from ensemble to principal, I had pretty much learned to take it all in stride. I simply reminded myself that it had nothing to do with my talent or ability, took what I could from the experience, and set my sights on the next opportunity. It's just what you do: You move on. You stay focused. You remain positive. You don't let it get to you.

Then one day you find yourself standing in a hallway sobbing.

~~~~~~~

It was fall 1985, and Nancy had booked me an audition for a new Howard Ashman/Marvin Hamlisch musical called *Smile*, an adaptation of the 1975 cult classic about the behind-the-scenes drama of a California beauty pageant.

As soon as Nancy told me, I flipped out. *A Chorus Line*—which Marvin composed the score for—was the first LP I ever bought, and at that point, *everyone* was talking about Howard's work on *Little Shop of Horrors*, so getting to work with both of them would be a dream come true.

The auditions were held at 890 Broadway, which consisted of several big, airy rehearsal studios located at—you guessed it—890 Broadway. As expected, when I arrived the waiting area was packed to the gills with aspiring twentysomething singers, many of whom I not only recognized but also knew by name.

Nancy had booked me a late-morning slot, and when I finally got called into the room, I caught poor Marvin in mid-bite as he was eating a massive pastrami sandwich. It was literally falling apart in his hands and making a mess all over the table. When he looked up at me, I got so flustered that I quickly blurted out an apology.

"I'm so sorry. My appointment came right during your lunch break, didn't it?"

God bless Marvin; he just smiled and assured me, "It's no problem. I can eat and listen at the same time."

And sure enough, he ate all the way through my audition, bits of shaved pastrami dropping everywhere. But the guy had three Academy Awards and four Grammys, and he had worked with Barbra Streisand on both *Funny Girl* and *The Way We Were*. I had been playing and singing along to his music since I was a kid. If he had asked, I probably would have run out and brought him back some mustard.

Howard, on the other hand, was a little more intense. He sat on the edge of his seat the entire time, meticulously taking notes like a man on a mission. In fairness, he was wearing a lot of hats. He was not only the lyricist but also the director and the book writer, which was pretty unusual—unless you're Howard Ashman.

It was—hands down—the most exciting and unnerving audition I'd ever had. The whole time I was singing, all I could think was, *Oh, please, God, let me get this. I want to work with these guys so much.*

I had picked the song "The Story Goes On" from *Baby*, a musical that had just finished a successful run on Broadway. The character who sang it, Lizzie, was roughly the same age (late teens) as most of the principal leads in *Smile*, and it was in the right vocal range (a high belt). Plus, like most of the lyrics Howard had written for *Little Shop*, it had a bit of a story to it, so I figured it was as good an audition piece as I was going to find.

And guess what? I got a callback. They wanted me to read for a character named Doria Hudson, one of the two main pageant contestants. According to the write-up, she is a headstrong, independent young woman whose parents split up when she was around 11, and she's now living in a tiny trailer halfway across the country from where she grew up, working the pageant circuit and dreaming about living at—of all places—Disneyland.

I'm going to pause for a second to let that sink in . . .

Well, the first callback went really well.

As did the second.

And the third.

I'm going to pause for a second to let that sink in . . .

Now it was obvious from the start that Howard was absolutely brilliant. He was also very hands-on and knew exactly what he wanted. At the top of the list? He wanted an actress who could sing, not a singer who could act. Why? Because that's how he wrote his lyrics. The whole play revolves around the individual journeys of the girls in the pageant, providing a wonderful through line of where each character starts, where she ends up, everything she learns, and everything she goes through. The songs are just the by-product of the script. When taking on one of these characters, you don't stop acting and start singing as much as you get to a place where there is no other way to express yourself *but* through song. It is all very fluid, taking the audience along on a lyrical journey without them even realizing it. Obviously, once the orchestra comes underneath with underscoring, you know a song is coming up, but the music connects everything together so beautifully that it all feels perfectly natural. The first time I heard Howard communicate that, I knew I had to work with him. He was a true actor's director—probably because he had been an actor himself. I don't know how else to explain it. He just . . . *got it*.

Which brings me to callback number four. It was an all-day sing-off, dance-off kind of thing, and it was horrible. By this point, I had already read several times, learned a few dance routines, and sung my heart out. I honestly didn't know what else I could possibly do. I was just emotionally exhausted, and despite my best effort to keep it together, it must have showed.

We were in a large rehearsal studio, and Mary Kyte, the choreographer, was teaching us yet another dance combination. Howard was sitting in the back watching and taking notes as usual. I was in the front line, right in front of the mirror, and I must have had that look that says, *I don't think I can do this anymore*—because right in the middle of the routine, Howard got up and walked over to the door. He pointed at me and waved me over.

My heart sank. I thought, *Oh no, here we go.* Desperately hoping nobody else had noticed (which, of course, they all had), I stepped out of the line and headed dejectedly toward the door.

Just don't start crying. Don't. Start. Crying.

Needless to say, as soon as I got into the hallway, I started crying.

"Why are you crying?" he asked.

"It's okay," I said, wiping my cheeks. "I know . . . I've been struggling. Just say it."

"Say what?" He seemed genuinely confused.

I just stared at the floor. "That I've been cut."

"No, you haven't."

What? I looked back up. The poor guy appeared about as shattered as I felt.

"I just couldn't watch you go through this anymore." Then he put his hands on my shoulders, lowered his head, and said, "Sweetie, you've already got the part."

"Are you kidding me?"

"No, I'm not," he said, chuckling. "We decided a couple days ago. You are Doria."

At that point, I just lost it and collapsed into Howard's arms, sobbing. And God bless him, he just held me and let me get it all out—all four callbacks' worth. After I had cried myself out, he looked at me and said, "Now, why don't you pull yourself together, go back in there, and have fun."

I wiped my nose and nodded. Then just before he opened the door, he turned to me and whispered, "And Jodi . . . just keep this to yourself, okay?"

Gosh, I loved that guy.

That was one of the kindest things anyone's ever done for me. And the truth is, he didn't have to do it. He could have just as easily let me finish the audition and wait for the final cast to be announced. But he didn't. He knew how hard I'd been working and how much this role meant to me. He also knew from experience how stressful the audition process could be—and I'm talking about the typical audition process. Four callbacks for a principal role was very much out of the ordinary. In fact, I'm fairly certain union rules prohibit that kind of thing now—or at the very least, I think that if they ask you to come back more than twice, they have to pay you for your time. Regardless, what Howard did that day was incredibly gracious and thoughtful. It was the kind of gesture that made him not only a wonderful director, but also a wonderful friend.

We all have the capacity to make someone else's life a little easier from time to time. And it doesn't require any special talent or skill—just a little compassion.

Howard didn't do anything extraordinary. Something just clicked in him that afternoon and he thought, *This isn't right. This poor girl shouldn't have to go through this.* And he did something about it.

Actually, now that I think about it, it *was* kind of extraordinary—maybe not to him, but it most definitely was to me. That's the beautiful thing about compassion. It takes so very little to give, and yet it means so very much.

One of my favorite Bible verses describes it as "a simple,

rule-of-thumb guide for behavior." You simply "ask your-self what you want people to do for you, then grab the initiative and do it for *them*."[1] That's all Howard did that day. He treated me the way he would have wanted to be treated. And really . . . how hard is *that*?

I'm just going to pause for a second to let that sink in.

11

"*No Time Will Be Better*"

What can I say about Doria Hudson?

She was my first starring role, and that alone will always give her a special place in my heart. But that's not the only reason I love her. She's such an endearing character—hopelessly insecure, desperately seeking the unconditional love she never got at home, and totally going about it in the wrong way. For her, beauty pageants are a way to feel valued and accepted. They give her a sense of identity. And God bless her, she genuinely believes she can live at Disneyland. Her story is so sad and yet so sweet. She's like a little girl trapped in a woman's body. On the outside, she's incredibly confident, outgoing, brassy, bossy, and when she needs it, a little bit spicy. But it's all just an act. On the inside, she's just a frightened, broken child.

That's what makes Howard's "Disneyland" so heart-wrenching. It's Doria's "I want" song, and even though people keep telling her everything at the park is made of "plywood and paste,"[1] she doesn't care. She still believes it's better than any place she's ever been. And these pageants? They're her ticket to get there.

I went to Disney World only once as a kid. I was around 10 or 11, and one summer Mom piled my cousins and me into the car and drove us down to Florida. I honestly don't remember much about it. But I could still see so much of myself in Doria—the broken home, the insecurity, the self-doubt, the longing for unconditional love, the dreams of escaping to a different place. For her it was Disneyland. For me it was Broadway.

That's the key to making a character work: You've got to find some of you in them. It's the only way your performance will ever be real, vulnerable, and authentic. You don't want to just present a character; you want to embody that person. And for a few magical hours each night, as much as possible, you need to become them. That's also the key to making a song work—especially Howard's. You've got to find a personal connection to it—some way to tell a story that's not only theirs, but also yours. In this case, I was lucky. In a lot of ways, I *was* Doria Hudson.

Of course, to Marvin, I would always be . . .

"Maserati!"

"It's Marzorati." I swear, that guy could never get my name right.

"Just come over here," he said with a laugh. "I wanna run through 'Disneyland' again."

"You know, Marvin," I teased back, "you really do need to learn how to pronounce my name."

He just sat at the piano and rolled his eyes.

"Marzorati. *M-A-R-*"

"Yeah, yeah." He waved me off, smiling. "By the way, you're gonna have to change that."

Is he serious?

"Are you serious?"

"Yes, I'm serious."

Guess he was serious.

"Why?"

"Well, first of all, it's too long. I can't spell it. I can't pronounce it. And I don't think anybody else is going to be able to either."

I had *no* words.

"What, you've never thought about it?" he asked.

I shook my head. I honestly hadn't. Even though Ray and I had been married for more than a year, I had kept my maiden name on all my headshots and résumés. It was just easier. Plus, at this stage of the game, I didn't want to risk losing what little name recognition I already had.

"Well, start thinking about it," he said, turning his attention back to his music, "because we're not putting 'Maserati' on the posters."

"Marzorati."

"Just change it, okay? Now let's go . . . from the top."

As much as I hated to admit it, Marvin had a point. This was my first starring role on Broadway, so my name would appear on the posters and publicity pieces. If ever I was going to change my name, now was definitely the time. But to what?

It turns out that Marvin was one step ahead of me. At the end of the day, he called the entire cast together and issued a proclamation: The next morning, everyone would write a last name on a slip of paper and toss it into a bowl, and whichever one I pulled out (assuming Marvin could spell and pronounce it) would be my stage name.

I know. What could possibly go wrong, right?

That night I filled Ray in on Marvin's little plan.

"Is he serious?"

"Oh . . . he's serious."

Ray thought about it for a minute, then said, "Well, I suppose if you were ever going to do it, now would be the time. But really? You're just gonna pick something out of a hat?"

"Actually, I think it's gonna be a bowl." At least I was focusing on the important bit.

He just laughed and said, "Okay, then. I hope you pick a winner."

To be honest, I was a little surprised Ray didn't just ask me to use his last name. I mean, technically, I was Jodi Benson. I know he was just being diplomatic. He knew how the business worked. But why couldn't I just . . . *Huh.* Why couldn't I?

The next day when I got to rehearsal, everyone was gathered around the bowl, laughing and tossing in little folded-up slips of paper. I glanced over a few people's shoulders as they were writing, and mostly they had come up with standard, easy-to-pronounce names like Thompson, Smith, Johnson . . .

Jodi Johnson?

Then when nobody was looking, I snatched a piece of paper, quickly scribbled my choice down, folded it, and hid it in my hand. After everyone had finished throwing their slips into the bowl, Marvin gave it a good shake and brought it over to me.

"All right, Maserati. Let's see what you get."

I stuck my hand in, rooted around a little, and pulled my hand back out holding the slip that had been tucked between my fingers the entire time.

"So, what's your new name?" Marvin asked.

"Oh," I chirped, feigning surprise. "It's Benson."

"Benson." Marvin chewed it over for a second. "Huh. I like it. It's easy to spell, easy to pronounce, and at the beginning of the alphabet, which'll put you right at the top for billing. I think it works!" Then he set the bowl down on the piano, put his hand on my shoulder, turned to the rest of the cast, and in very dramatic fashion, announced, "Ladies and gentlemen . . . I give you—Jodi Benson."

After a polite round of applause, Howard and Mary stepped in and got the ball rolling on rehearsal while Marvin dumped the rest of the names into the trash. As I was heading out the door after rehearsal, he called out, "Night, Benson. Good job today."

"Thanks." Then I stopped and turned around. "By the way . . . Marvin?"

"Yeah?"

"I played a little bit of a joke on you today."

"Oh?"

"Yeah. Benson? That's Ray's last name. I had the slip in my hand the entire time."

He just stared at me for a second. Then his mouth curved into a smile, and he laughed and said, "Well, good call, Benson. It's a great name."

Yeah, it is.

When I got home, Ray was waiting. "So how did it go?"

"It went great," I said, dropping my backpack on the futon before plopping down next to it.

"Well . . . ?" he asked. "What's the new name?"

"Hmm? Oh . . . Benson," I said casually.

I wish you could have seen the look on his face. It was like someone had just asked a four-year-old if he'd like to have some ice cream and then go to the puppy store.

"Seriously? You mean someone actually—"

"I did." I couldn't help but smile. Ray's expression was just too priceless. "I had it all planned from the start. I wrote it down on a slip of paper when I got there, and then I hid it in my hand."

"You what?"

"Come on, Ray. There was no way I was going to pull any name but yours out of that bowl."

By that point, Ray's eyes had completely filled with tears. I don't know that I'd ever seen him quite so touched.

And do you know what? It felt so good seeing "Jodi Benson" on that poster.

And why wouldn't it? It's who I am.

~~~~~~~~~

The fact that Doria and I have a lot in common definitely helped my performance, but in some ways, we are also worlds apart. For one thing, Doria is far more comfortable using her "assets" and playing up her sensuality than I will ever be. She knows how to sell it, and even if I could, I would never feel comfortable enough to try. It's just not me.

She also strikes me as someone who wouldn't be afraid to step on a few toes to get what she wants. I don't think she'd ever do anything horrible, but I can definitely see her talking some smack, and that's never been my thing either.

The biggest distinction, though, is that Doria finds her identity mostly in physical things—her looks; her standing in the pageant circuit; her talents, titles, and tiaras. Mine is found in my faith. I'm a child of the King, and my identity is in Him. Jesus challenges His followers to be light and salt—to add illumination and flavor to a dark world so that people can flourish. I want to be someone who brings out the "God-flavors" and "God-colors in this world," as Eugene Peterson puts it.[2] I want people to see that God is the source of all love and beauty. I'm just here for a season to make a positive difference however I can—not for my own glory or recognition, but for His. Simply put, my job is to walk my talk—to build people up and make sure they feel seen and heard, whether it's for three minutes at a meet and greet or every day at home.

It's a dangerous and slippery slope when your identity begins to get tied up in what you do, who you know, or how you look. Looks fade. Jobs come and go. People come in and out of your life. Then what do you do? Who are you?

I love playing Ariel. I always have, and I always will. But it's not who I am. It's just one of the many avenues God has given me to make a positive impact on others for Him. It's not about me; it's about something so much bigger. Something that's never going to change, never going to crumble, and never going to disappear. And it's not just a fantasy or a daydream. It's real.

Now that I think about it, there's one other thing Doria and I have in common: We both have teachable spirits. I had Ray, Pastor Ed, and Juanita speaking into my life and helping me figure out who and what I wanted to be. Doria's closest confidant in *Smile* is her roommate, Robin. Unlike Doria, Robin comes from a very tight-knit, loving family. She's bright, she's caring, and she really doesn't want anything to do with the pageant circuit. The only reason she's there is because her mom thinks it would be a great opportunity for her to make some friends and build her self-esteem. What makes Robin and Doria such a fun pair is that they are polar opposites. Doria represents everything Robin wishes she could be—popular, outgoing, and confident—and Doria sees in Robin everything she always wanted to have—stability and a loving family that genuinely cares about her and supports her.

Anyway, by the end of the second act, Doria realizes she doesn't have an ice cube's chance of winning the competition, but Robin does. And that's when something amazing happens. For the first time in her life, Doria puts someone else's interests before her own and channels all her energy into building up Robin's confidence, getting her to realize just how special she is, and helping her win.

I'm not going to spoil the ending. Actually, I am. Neither of them wins. Well, not the pageant anyway. But if you ask me, I think they both walk away with something even better.

Robin goes home to her family more confident and—thanks to Doria—with a better understanding of and appreciation for who she is. And thanks to Robin, Doria has grown from someone who is completely self-absorbed to someone who is capable of caring about somebody else more than she cares about herself. She still has a long way to go, but she's taken an important first step.

It just goes to show that anyone can change. You just have to figure out who you really want to be.

12

"*If You Keep On Believing...*"

Everybody has a favorite Disney movie. Growing up, mine was *Cinderella*. Wicked stepsisters, a fairy godmother, a charming prince, mice that can sew—what's *not* to love? I think what I liked most about it, though, was Cinderella's undying belief that no matter how grim her situation appeared, everything would somehow work out in the end. She never let her circumstances get her down. She just stayed positive, kept her head up, and continued to dream. Sometimes that's all you can do.

Smile had all the characteristics of a great fairy tale—a wonderful story, a great cast, and of course, Howard and Marvin. From day one, the expectations for the show were through the roof—so much so that *60 Minutes* sent Diane Sawyer to do a feature on it. She and her team followed us

around, filming rehearsals, interviewing the cast, profiling
the producers, and documenting every celebratory step and
bump in the road. I know . . . nothing like a little added
pressure, right?

Granted, the lion's share of the pressure landed squarely
on Howard's and Marvin's shoulders. After all, Marvin
was already a Broadway icon, so naturally, everyone just
assumed *Smile* was going to be his next big tour de force.
And even though Howard was relatively new to the scene,
he had already made quite a splash himself with *Little Shop of
Horrors*. Put the two of them together and you got . . . well,
as it turned out, a lot of tension.

Howard and Marvin were both brilliant, but they had
wildly different personalities. Marvin was loud, brash—the
picture of confidence and bravado. There wasn't a question in his mind about whether *Smile* was going to be a
runaway success. I remember one time we were rehearsing
"Disneyland," and he stopped right in the middle of it,
smiled at me, and said, "You just might get a Tony Award
for this." I laughed it off. I mean, it was nice of him to say,
and I know he was just joking, but still . . . it's kind of an
unwritten rule in the theatre—you don't talk like that. But
that's just the way Marvin was. He was constantly saying
things like "I could see us winning Best Musical" or "You
and Ray might even be able to buy your first house with
this show!"

Howard, on the other hand, was much more pragmatic.
He didn't make grand predictions or promises. He just did
his job. He'd come up onstage, we'd talk about what Doria
would be feeling at different moments during her songs, and
then he'd help me figure out the best way to convey that.

He'd give feedback like "I need you to hold back on this bit. I don't want you to start crying. Don't even let a single tear drop down. I just want you to take it to the very edge of tears so we can feel what you're feeling, but without actually letting it go." That kind of stuff. All Howard cared about was putting on a great show, and after that, whatever happened, happened.

And frankly I was with him. I mean, I'd had high hopes for *Marilyn*, and that had closed in two weeks. That's just the nature of the business. All it takes is one bad review to bring the curtain down for good, and nobody—not even the great Marvin Hamlisch—was immune to that.

The weird thing is, in musical theatre, a writing partnership is a lot like a marriage. Marvin already had a wildly successful partnership going with Carole Bayer Sager, and Howard had done both *Little Shop* and *God Bless You, Mr. Rosewater* with Alan Menken, so I have no idea who matched the two of them up—or why—but it was not a good blend. They were just like oil and water, and the deeper we got into the process, the worse the tension got.

The first cracks started to show early on when financial backers David Geffen and the Shubert Organization both pulled out of the show after the first workshop. That was big. The Shubert Organization owned 16 theatres in the Broadway District, including the Shubert Theatre, which, at that point, had housed *A Chorus Line* for a decade. Their lack of confidence struck a huge blow to Marvin and also left *Smile* without a theatre to call home.

Cue the backers' auditions.

A backers' audition is basically a condensed dog and pony show that you present to a group of investors, hoping they'll get behind the show. We did several of them all over the country. The good news was, we came away with a lot of financial partners and producers. The bad news was, we came away with *a lot* of financial partners and producers. It was like *Marilyn* all over again—a whole bunch of cooks in the kitchen, all of whom had strong opinions about what needed to happen to get the show ready for opening night. And opening night was still a *long* way off. First, we had to get through Baltimore.

Why Baltimore? Well, after you've secured backing, a Broadway show generally does at least one out-of-town tryout. It's usually in a major city like Los Angeles, Denver, or Chicago. Ours was in Baltimore because that was Howard's hometown. These performances are really taxing because you're doing five to six hours of rehearsal during the day, followed by a live performance that evening. The next morning, when you show up for rehearsal you'll find a new version of the script. Everything is up for grabs and constantly changing—dialogue, songs, choreography, sometimes entire scenes. One night they might take something out, and two days later they might put it back in, only slightly different. It's just exhausting, and our tryout went on for six weeks.

That was when the rift between Howard and Marvin hit its peak. Now, of course they were very professional about it. It's not as if they were having full-on knock-down, drag-out fights or shouting matches in front of us, but you could hear it in their tone and you could see it in their body language—the way they'd abruptly turn and walk away from each other after a discussion. They just were not getting along, and after a while, we all started to feel the strain.

Honestly, if it hadn't been for my dear friend Cindy Oakes

Miller, I don't know if I would have made it. Cindy played one of the other pageant contestants, Connie-Sue Whipple. Her "talent" was, of all things, twirling a flaming baton while on pointe (up on her toes). Thank goodness I didn't get that part. Cindy, however, was brilliantly cast. She was not only a wonderful ballerina but could also actually twirl. She could throw a baton 10 feet up in the air and catch it without batting an eyelash. As for the fire part . . . well, let's just say the fire marshal was none too pleased about the prospect of the theatre going up in flames one night—to music, no less. If I recall correctly, Howard was able to win him over by agreeing to have stage managers standing by with fire extinguishers and buckets full of sand whenever Cindy was doing her thing. Because that's what *Smile* was lacking at that point—more drama.

Anyway, in addition to being incredibly talented, Cindy was also a believer, and we latched on to each other from day one. We lived only a few blocks apart, so we would ride our bikes back and forth to the theatre every day. We also roomed together in Baltimore. It was a real blessing to have a like-minded person in the cast to help keep me focused and grounded. Just having her there as a spiritual support made all the difference in the world.

I'd never had a starring role before, and it really did feel different. It seemed like there was a lot more riding on me than usual, not only from a performance perspective, but personally as well—as though others were watching to see how I was handling the chaos, and then taking their cues from me. And believe me, I was struggling just like everybody else. But Cindy was so encouraging. Whenever she sensed I was getting ready to snap, she would gently pull me aside and say, "Jodi, you're doing your best. In fact, you're doing great. And that's all you *can* do. Marvin and Howard and everything else—that's out of our hands. All we can do is be light and salt."

That was a big thing to us, being light and salt—showing others the same love and kindness that God shows to us. For the most part, our cast got along amazingly well, but whenever you get a bunch of people together day in, day out in that kind of pressure cooker environment, you're going to have some challenges. Cindy and I tried to steer clear of the drama and focus our energy on building each other up and being as positive, encouraging, and supportive as possible. And wow, did we need each other, because as tense as things were in Baltimore, they got even worse when we came back to New York.

With only 10 days to go until opening night, the billboards were up, the marquee had been set, the promotional posters were plastered all over the front of the Lunt-Fontanne Theatre, and we were *still* making adjustments. Major ones. The show was just not coming together. Meanwhile, in one corner we had Marvin telling Diane Sawyer that everything was great and the production was going to be a huge hit, and in the other we had Howard essentially telling us, "Oh, my gosh, people . . . we don't know what the heck we're doing." I pretty much knew at that point it was going to take a miracle to make this show work.

Fortunately, that's exactly what we got.

Opening night was a fantastic success. Cindy didn't burn the place to the ground, and the audience was jumping to their feet, hooting and hollering all night. It was a lovefest. Opening nights usually are—in part because the audience is packed with friends and family of the cast and crew. There are plenty of tickets left over for the general public and a handful of critics, but for the most part, opening night really is a houseful of joy and celebration—as well it should be after so many months of hard work.

I'm not ashamed to admit I had my own little cheering section out there. My mom, stepdad, sister-in-law, and niece all flew in for the show. Obviously Ray was there, too, clapping his hands raw along with a bunch of our friends from New York. I used every free ticket they gave me and still ended up buying a few extras. But it was worth it to look out during the final curtain call and see everyone who'd been there from the beginning smiling back at me.

After the show, we got all dolled up, piled into a herd of waiting limousines, and headed over to Studio 54 for the after-party, where, if memory serves me correctly, I exhaled for the first time in almost a year. It felt so good to finally relax and just enjoy spending time with my family and friends without the specter of opening night hanging over my head.

We hung out, ate our weight in hors d'oeuvres, and then, just as Ray and I were heading to the dance floor, a gentleman I didn't recognize stepped up to the podium, grabbed a mic, and said, "Ladies and gentlemen, we have a very special surprise guest here tonight, and he's got some wonderful news to deliver. Would Jodi and Anne Marie please come to the stage."

I turned to Ray and mouthed, *What is this?* but he just shrugged, looking every bit as confused as I was.

Once my friend Anne Marie, who played Robin, and I got to the stage, the announcer told us to close our eyes. Why? I had no idea. Then I felt someone come up behind me. I turned around, opened my eyes, and almost passed out.

Standing there, right in front of me, close enough to touch, was Mickey Mouse. I mean, the actual Mickey Mouse. I totally flipped out.

"Good evening, Mickey," the announcer broke back in. "I believe you have a special presentation to make."

Mickey nodded his head and turned toward me.

What's happening?

The next thing I knew, two giant white-gloved hands were handing me a beautiful gold embossed plaque that read,

DISNEYLAND HONORARY CITIZEN

Whereas you are entering a world where
happiness is a way of life,

where the young of heart of all ages can
forget their everyday cares; and

Whereas you can now share the
imagination, enchantment, adventure
and laughter that have been wrought by Disneyland,

Let it be known by this document that the title of

"Honorary Citizen of Disneyland"

is bestowed upon you,

Jodi Benson
This 24th day of November 1986
Mickey Mouse

I was speechless. I mean, what do you say when the Big Mouse himself hands you the keys to the Magic Kingdom? I had been an emotional, blubbering mess all day, and now this? I knew it was just because of the song "Disneyland," but still . . .

It was the perfect ending to a perfect day—Doria's dream had finally come true, and after months of anxiety, stress, and frustration, I felt like an honest-to-goodness princess for one magical evening.

Of course, as so often happens in fairy tales, right around midnight . . .

Frank Rich's review came out. Yep, the same guy who single-handedly shut down *Marilyn*. We all knew it was coming. Frank was always at opening night, and with all the hype surrounding *Smile*, there was no way he was going to miss this one.

Here's the thing about an opening night review: If it's a rave, either the director or one of the producers will gather everyone around and read it out loud at the after-party—and that's when the celebration really kicks into high gear. But if it's bad, the party just kind of winds down. There's no grand announcement—just telltale whispers followed by awkward silence.

Shortly after the clock struck 12, the whispers started. Looking around the room, I saw a handful of people holding early copies of the morning paper. All of them had the same hollow, shell-shocked look. And Howard and Marvin were nowhere to be found.

Ray turned to me, a solemn expression on his face, and asked, "Do you want me to get a copy?"

I just shook my head. "Why bother? There's nothing I can do about it."

"Do you want to leave?"

I thought about it for a second, then shook my head

again. "No. I wanna stay. Mom and Jill are both here, and all our friends . . . I'm not going to let one lousy review ruin everyone's night. Let's just enjoy it."

"Are you sure?" he asked, taking my hand.

"Yeah . . . I'm sure."

We stayed a while longer, but the mood had clearly shifted. And you know, I don't think I ever saw Marvin again after that. I don't think anybody did. He just went into hiding. A few weeks later, when I finally got around to reading the review, I understood why. It was pretty brutal.

Honestly, that's why I don't read them. Not only won't it change anything, but you also still have to go out and perform the next night. What positive fruit could possibly come from filling your head with someone else's negative opinions? Because at the end of the day, that's all it is—one person's opinion.

Of course, in this case, it was a powerful opinion. The minute that paper went to press, the writing was on the wall. It was only a matter of time.

It's at that point your mind immediately shifts from *Huh . . . maybe I could get a Tony for this* to *Oh, my gosh, how am I going to pay the rent?* The second you get home, you call your agent and say, "Hey, it looks like I'm going to be available here pretty soon." Then you ask them to start putting out feelers and lining up auditions. In our case, the timing was terrible—we opened right before Thanksgiving, and the holidays are always a tricky time to try to find another job. You kinda have to wait for the next season of shows to come around, which means you could be unemployed for a while.

The next evening, when we got to the theatre, Howard

called everyone together and pretty much confirmed what we already knew.

"Well, it is what it is. I'm so sorry. I know this is hard. I know it's painful. But we did our best. There's nothing more we can do. Just keep putting on the best show you can, and we'll do what we can to keep the doors open."

From that point on, our lives revolved around Tuesdays. That was the day the notice went up on the call-board letting us know how much longer we had a job. It was right next to the stage door, so we saw it the second we showed up for work:

The final performance of *Smile* will be on --------.

If the notice came down, it meant enough tickets had sold to keep the doors open for another week. But it's expensive to keep a Broadway show open for a whole week, and few people would spend 50 to 60 dollars a pop to see something that's been poorly reviewed.

Our notice went up and down several times over the next few weeks, and those were some tough times. It's hard not to be all gloom and doom when you know you're about to lose your job. I tried to keep my sights set on the bigger picture of what God was doing. After all, it was just a job. Jobs come and go. If this season of *Smile* was going to last only a few weeks, I was going to make the most of it.

Everything is a stepping-stone to something else. God had given me this opportunity for a reason. I just needed to focus on doing my best work and making whatever time I had left a great experience for myself and the rest of the cast. My daily reminder to them was basically, "Look, I know this isn't what any of us wanted, but let's try to have fun and enjoy the ride for however long it lasts, 'cause we're never gonna have this chance or this time together again." Still, it was hard.

I did get a little bit of an emotional boost when Disney's Jeffrey Katzenberg, Michael Eisner, and Peter Schneider stopped by my dressing room after the show one night. They had come to see Howard, who had recently signed on to do a new project for their studio—some animated film about a mermaid. Apparently Howard had been talking to the powers that be about a new way of doing animated features— more in the style of a Broadway musical—so they all flew out to New York to see what it was all about.

Jeffrey, Michael, and Peter were incredibly kind and very complimentary. They told me how much they enjoyed the show and my performance, especially "Disneyland." By that point, I was thrilled to hear that somebody liked it—and that Howard had another job lined up. The guy was so incredibly talented. For that matter, so was Marvin. All of us were. Frank's review might have killed our ticket sales, but it didn't take anything away from *us*—nothing that mattered, anyway.

As December wore on, the notices continued to go up and down, and by the grace of God, we were able to keep the doors open through Christmas. But sure enough, as soon as the holidays were over, there it was:

> After the final performance on January 3,
> the production of *Smile* will officially be closed.

"Do you think maybe we'll get another week?" I asked hopefully when I saw the sign. But the look on our stage manager's face told me everything I needed to know.

"I don't think so." He sighed apologetically. "I think this is it."

That was disheartening. After more than a year's worth of backers' auditions, rehearsals, and preview shows, it was all over in six weeks.

I swear, someday I'm gonna do something Frank Rich actually likes.

Later that week, Ray and I rang in the New Year, hoping and praying for good things to come, and two days later, the *Smile* cast gave our final performance.

It was bittersweet. I loved everybody in the cast, and despite all the tension and frustration, it had been a wonderful experience. God used that season of my life in so many amazing ways. I mean, if it hadn't been for *Smile*, I wouldn't have met Cindy, who became a lifelong friend and prayer partner; I wouldn't have become "Jodi Benson"; and I wouldn't have met Howard. It just goes to show that God can make any situation fruitful. You just have to trust Him and keep on believing that the best is yet to come.

Just before the show closed down for good, Howard pulled me aside. I just assumed he was going to thank me for all my hard work and wish me the best moving forward. But Howard being Howard, he did me one better.

"Listen," he said, "I'm so sorry this didn't work out. You were great, and you deserve better."

The poor guy. I could see he felt terrible.

"I'm sure you've heard I've been working on a new project with Disney," he continued. "Well, we're going to need some actresses who can sing, so if you're interested, I'd be happy to arrange for you to get an audition."

He made the same offer to a few of the other girls as well. Seriously—the guy was a prince.

And that was it.

Smile was over.

I was out of a job.

And Howard was embarking on a new quest: scouring the countryside in search of a princess who could sing.

And in true fairy-tale fashion . . . guess who was holding the keys to the kingdom?

13

*"Strollin' Along down the . . .
What's That Word Again?"*

"I'm here for my 2:00 appointment," I whispered. "Jodi Benson."

The assistant gave her clipboard a quick scan. "Yes, Ms. Benson, go ahead and have a seat. We'll call you when we're ready."

"Thank you."

I quietly made my way down the hall lined with girls sitting on folding chairs, listening to their Walkmans and flipping through the same three-page write-up I'd been sent. I took a seat at the very end of the line and pulled out of my backpack the little folded-up character description my agent, Nancy, had sent me:

Ariel is an independent, headstrong, and determined young mermaid who sings, daydreams, and is willing

to risk everything to explore the shore above. Her
unflappable spirit and resilience carry her through
her journey of self-discovery, through which she
becomes a courageous young woman who discovers
her place in the world.

Independent, headstrong, determined, unflappable,
courageous—I adored Ariel from the moment I read that
description. The question was, what did all those qualities
sound like? I knew what they looked like—the posture, the
way you carried yourself onstage, the way you walked, facial
expressions, body language—but vocally? I had been playing
with different voices all week, and none of them felt quite
right.

I glanced back down the hall. *There are plenty of people
ahead of me yet. I wonder if . . .* I snuck a quick peek around
the corner. *Yep, there it is.* I quietly picked up my backpack
and slipped around the corner into the ladies' room.

"Hello?"

Nothing.

I did a quick check under all the stalls.

No feet.

Perfect.

I set my backpack on the little counter next to the sink
and dug out the sample pages of dialogue that had come with
the character description. It was a scene between Ariel and her
father, King Triton, and frankly, it read an awful lot like the
kind of arguments I'd had with my own parents growing up.

I looked in the mirror and in my best "headstrong" voice
announced, "I'm 16 years old. I'm not a child anymore!"

Gosh, does that sound 16?

I was 25. Maybe that was my problem. My natural speaking voice wasn't super deep, but it wasn't exactly "teenagery" either. I tried again, but this time in a slightly higher register, and it did sound younger; but then I wondered, *Does that sound independent?*

"I'm 16 years old—" *Nope. Maybe if I try it with my eyes closed?*

"I'm 16—" *Nope. Gosh, I have never been this hyper focused on my voice before.*

That's when it hit me . . .

Maybe I'm focusing on it too much.

Whenever Howard talked to me about Doria, he never once talked about her age (for the record, she was also 16). He talked about who she was, what she was feeling, and how she interpreted the world around her. Maybe if I could just get the attitude right, the voice would follow.

"I'm 16 years old. I'm not a child anymore." *Well . . . that's . . . I don't know.*

I just sighed and stuffed my lines into my backpack. *I'm just gonna go in there, give it a go, and whatever happens, happens. They won't pick me anyway. I don't know the first thing about voice-over work.*

I went back out, plopped down in my chair, and waited.

"Jodi Benson?" the girl with the clipboard called out. "You're up."

I smiled politely, walked over to the door, and went into the rehearsal studio expecting absolutely nothing. And that's pretty much what I found waiting for me—just a big, empty room with two chairs, a mic stand, and a little table with an old reel-to-reel tape machine on it. That, and—

"Albert!" Albert Tavares had been the assistant director

and casting director for *Smile*. He and Howard were really tight. He used to rehearse scenes with us and helped bring us up to speed on daily page changes during the Baltimore fiasco. He was such a sweet, gentle, soft-spoken, little guy. Gosh, I probably outweighed him by about 20 pounds. He would always sit at the front of the stage, legs crossed, a notepad and pen in his hands, and the sweetest expression on his face. He reminded me of Peter Pan, and I absolutely adored him.

"Jodi!" he said, beaming as he crossed the room to give me a hug. "I haven't seen you since the after-party."

"I know! Gosh, this is so great. I didn't know you were working on this." I instantly felt better.

He smiled, "Yeah, well, you know . . ."

We both laughed and said, "Howard."

"So." He clapped his hands together. "Are you ready?"

"As ready as I'll ever be."

Albert motioned toward the chair with the mic stand in front of it. "Great. Have a seat. You got the demo tape, right?"

"Mm-hmm." I nodded. In addition to the character description and the little snippets of dialogue, Disney had sent a cassette tape of Howard singing "Part of Your World" as his writing partner, Alan Menken, played the piano. That was our audition piece.

I must have listened to that tape a couple of dozen times over the previous week. I loved the song—especially the way Howard sang it. I spent the whole week trying to mimic everything he did. After all, this wasn't my first Ashman production. I knew what Howard wanted. He wasn't just singing "Part of Your World"; he was singing it the way he wanted it to be sung.

"All right, Jodi," Albert chirped, settling in behind the table. "Whenever you're ready."

When I nodded, Albert started up the reel-to-reel and flipped on a recording of Alan playing the piano accompaniment.

The second I started singing, all the weird fears and paranoias I had about my voice melted away, and I just lost myself in the song, so much so that I was a little thrown when Albert stopped me midway through.

"We're not doing the whole thing?" I asked.

"Nope," he said, resetting the tape. "Just enough to give them an idea of what you can do."

"Oh . . . was it okay?"

"Oh, you were great." Albert was so sweet. He probably said that to everyone. And you know what? It worked. I immediately felt calmer.

"Ready to try a few lines?"

Shoot. I had so much fun singing the song that I had almost forgotten about reading the script.

"Yep."

Albert restarted the reel-to-reel recorder and then read me in. I knew he was reading it straight and not actually acting it out, but there was just something so disarmingly adorable about mild-mannered Albert assuming the role of a larger-than-life, majestic, bellowing sea king.

We ran through the scene a couple of times, and each time Albert had me do it a little differently. I wasn't necessarily doing it wrong. Honestly, who could say at that point? I think he just wanted to get a couple of passes on tape that showed I could take direction.

That's really important. You can be incredibly talented,

but if you're not open to feedback or willing to shift your performance to fit the needs of the director or the production, you're not going to last very long in this business. Whenever I give a workshop or a master class, I stress that above all else, you want to be teachable, coachable, and directable. You don't want to be known as difficult. You want to show that you're resilient and flexible because those are the kinds of qualities directors look for.

From the very beginning, I've always thought of myself as a work-for-hire. The director tells me what he wants, and then I do everything I can to make it happen. Likewise, when I'm asked to give a concert, I don't come in with a set song list. I just ask whoever's in charge, "What would *you* like me to sing?" and we go from there. And even though I don't think I've ever done a performance that hasn't included "Part of Your World," I always sing it exactly the same way it sounds in the movie because I know that's what people want. They don't want to hear my interpretation of it. They want to hear Howard's interpretation of it—the one they know and love from the film.

Even at auditions where there was a lot at stake, I came in prepared, but I tried to be as flexible as possible. For example, if they said, "So what are you going to be doing for us today?" I would always leave the door open with, "Well, I've got this, this, and this. Which would you like to hear?" Or I'd just come right out and ask, "Is there anything you're sick to death of hearing today?" Then I'd make a point to do something else—not so much to stand out but to give them a bit of a break.

And if I happened to make a mistake, I owned it. I've made tons of them over the years. Whenever it happens,

I just laugh at myself and say, "Whoops, that was a clunker. Can I try that again?" At this stage of the game, they already know when someone has talent. Being willing to fess up to mistakes also shows a good sense of self-awareness and the ability not to take yourself too seriously.

Granted, sometimes things happen that can't be controlled. For example, the pianist may play in the wrong key or at the wrong tempo—and when that happens, you can't look over at them and say, "Oh, my gosh, you're destroying my audition." You have to keep going. It's not optimal, but it does demonstrate resilience, adaptability, and flexibility to the casting team. And that's important, because mistakes *do* happen in live theatre. What they want to know is, how are you going to handle it? Is it going to rock your world, or are you going to keep plowing forward? I learned early on that it's best to keep plowing forward without looking over at the pianist or showing any displeasure on your face. That lets everyone at the table know that your feathers don't ruffle easily.

Anyway, after Albert got several different passes on tape, he gave me the thumbs-up.

"Great job, Jodi. That was really good."

"Are you sure?" I asked. "Because I have no idea what I'm doing."

"No, no, no. It was great. I think you got the sense of the character, and it sounds like you got what Howard was doing with the song."

"Yeah, well . . . I basically imitated his version."

He just laughed. "Yep, Howard's pretty specific about what he wants."

"Oh yeah. I definitely know that." Yet another way God used *Smile* for good.

"So is that it, then?" I asked.

"Yep, that's it. We'll send these reels back to Disney, and they'll let you know."

By the time I'd walked back out of the studio after Albert and I said our goodbyes, the hall was filled with a completely new set of girls waiting for their shot. I made a point to stop and thank the assistant, made sure she had all the information she needed, and then headed back home.

I still didn't think I had any chance of getting the part, but at least I'd been able to see Albert again, and that alone made the audition worth it. From that time on, it was all in God's hands.

~~~~~~

Call me. Nancy.

I looked up from my pager to see where I was. *Hmm . . . 16th and Broadway. I think there's a phone booth down there.* As I made my way along the crowded sidewalk, I reached back and grabbed the bottom of my backpack to make sure I still had a roll of quarters tucked away.

Yep. Good thing it's laundry day.

After entering a nearby phone booth, I pulled the door shut to drown out as much of the street noise as possible and dialed Nancy's number.

"Bret Adams, Limited. May I help you?"

"Yes, hi, this is Jodi Benson returning Nancy's page."

"Hold on, please."

Within seconds, Nancy's cheery voice came on the line. "Hey, sweetie, how are you?"

"I'm good, thanks. I was just on my way to a voice lesson and saw your page. What's up?"

"Well, I just got the call from Disney, and you got it!"

"Got *what?*"

"You're Ariel."

Ariel? Who's Ariel?

"I'm not quite . . . gosh, *what* is that from? What is it?"

"Remember that animated film Howard Ashman was doing?"

"Oh yeah, yeah, yeah. That audition that I did with Albert. That was—what—a year ago?"

"Well, you got it. You got the part!"

"Oh, my gosh, that's incredible!" Unbelievable was more like it. *Why in the world would they go with me? I don't know anything about voice-over work.*

"Congrats, sweetie. As soon as I get the final contract from Disney, I'll give you a call, and you can come down and sign everything." She went on to say something about the recording taking place in LA and the Disney team handling all the travel arrangements, but at that point my head was swimming so frantically I could barely understand English.

Seriously, how did I get this part?

Granted, there was never any question in my mind that I was going to do it. I'd be insane not to. For one thing, it was a job, and Disney was . . . well, Disney. I had no idea what it was like to actually work for them, but if the three execs who stopped by my dressing room after the *Smile* performance that night were any indication, it promised to be a fantastic experience. And of course, it meant I was going to get another chance to work with Howard. There was no way I was going to miss out on that. Still . . .

Ahhh, let it go, Jodi.

I might not have known anything about voice-over work,

but clearly *something* about my audition tape told them I could do it. And I know it wasn't Howard's doing because there weren't any names or faces attached to the demo reels. They wouldn't have even known whose was whose until they'd made their decision, and that's assuming Howard even got a vote. Besides, I could have sworn Albert mentioned that Ron Clements and John Musker, the directors, were going to be making the final call, and I'd never met either of them.

I mean, seriously, what were the odds that out of more than 400 girls, many of whom I'm sure had more voice-over experience than I did, I would get this part?

In my mind, there was only one explanation.

After Nancy and I said our goodbyes, I stepped out of that little phone booth and headed back down Broadway to my voice lesson. And despite all my festering insecurities, deep inside I felt a strange sense of confidence that I knew could come from only one source—the same One I credited with getting me the job in the first place.

An Old Testament prophet said, "Whether you turn to the right or to the left, your ears will hear a voice behind you, saying, 'This is the way; walk in it.'"[1] I love that. Taking a break from Broadway to do voice-over work certainly wasn't the career path I had been following at that point, but clearly God saw things differently. And if He wanted me to veer off to the right for a season, that's what I was going to do.

I think God is looking for people who are flexible and can take a little direction too. None of us are perfect, and He knows there's always room for improvement. The question is, when God presents you with an opportunity to step outside your comfort zone and do something that's not necessarily your thing, what are you going to do with it? Are you going to let it rock your world, or are you just going to keep plowing forward?

Me? I opted to keep plowing forward.

And wow, did it ever rock my world.

14

"Don't Underestimate the Importance of Body Language"

Believe it or not, I have a lot of friends who don't really know what I do for a living. And do you know what? I am totally fine with that.

When I was first cast as Ariel, almost every time I told somebody about it, they would get this pitiful expression and say something like, "Oh, that's too bad. You're doing a cartoon"—as if my entire career had just tanked. So I just stopped telling people. I figured nobody would find out about it anyway. Back then voice-over actors didn't typically get front-end billing—just a quick acknowledgment during the closing credits as everyone filed out of the theatre. Of course, after the movie came out, everyone was all, "Why didn't you tell me?" But up until then, as far as most people were concerned, my career had pretty much gone down the toilet.

Obviously, things are much different now. Thanks to people like Angela Lansbury, Robin Williams, James Earl Jones, and Tom Hanks, voice-over work has garnered a whole new level of respect. But in the mid-eighties, it was still largely looked down upon by the New York theatre community. People just assumed that live theatre was far more demanding, both physically and emotionally. After all, you're out there working your tail off—singing, dancing, and acting—eight shows a week. All that voice-over people do is sit in a chair behind a microphone and talk, right?

Wrong.

Having done both, I can promise you, voice-over work is every bit as physically taxing and emotionally draining as stage acting—sometimes more so. You don't have the advantage of using your body or facial expressions to help you communicate, so you have to get everything across using only your voice. It's exhausting because you're not just sitting behind a mic—at least I'm not. I'm up on my feet acting everything out as I go, sometimes for eight hours straight. There are days I've walked out of the recording studio dripping with sweat and wanting to lie down for a while. It can take dozens of passes to get a single line right, and depending on what you're doing—singing, shouting, sobbing—it can really take a toll on your voice.

And if you've never done it before, wow, is there ever a learning curve.

My first full day in the recording studio for *The Little Mermaid* was a symphony of errors. For one thing, I kept smacking the mic (and the mic stand and the sheet music). I couldn't help it. I'm half Italian and have a tendency to talk with my hands, which does not play well in a professional recording studio, where the microphones are unbelievably sensitive. Even when I managed to miss hitting the mic, the guys in the control room still picked up the whoosh of air as my hands went by. They were always very sweet about it. They'd just smile and say, "Let's try that one again," but I can't imagine it didn't get on their nerves in a *What the heck is she doing?* kind of way.

And then of course, there was the other matter. When you're singing for long stretches, you end up drinking a lot of water. It keeps your mouth, throat, and vocal cords moist and makes it easier to articulate and to sing clearly. Unfortunately, it also makes you belch—a lot. I don't know how many times I made those poor guys wait while I tried to get it all out of my system before we started recording again. The kicker is, they were *always* recording. As a result, I'm sure if they wanted to, someone over at Disney could probably still blackmail me with a hidden "Benson burp track."

If that wasn't enough, I kept oversinging. Everything was too big, too loud, too much. I was the vocal equivalent of a bull in a china shop. Fortunately, the entire team was incredibly gracious and accommodating.

Once, after we had spent several hours laying down passes of "Part of Your World," the guys in the control room realized there was a problem with one of the mics, and we ended up losing everything we had done that day. By that point, I was starting to get self-conscious about all the mistakes I'd been making, and I was feeling burned-out and a little frustrated. For whatever reason, it just wasn't clicking. I wasn't in the moment, and Howard could see it, so he very wisely said, "Why don't we take a break. When we come back, we're going to try something different, okay?"

I stepped out of the recording studio and went to the ladies' room to splash a little cold water on my face. When I returned, Howard had turned off all the lights in the studio and control room. The only illumination came from the faint glow of the reading light on my music stand.

Apparently, while I was out, Howard had said, "We need to change things up a little here. She's a Broadway girl, a theatre person. We've got to create a different kind of space for her, because having her stand here and sing in a fully lit room with everybody staring at her from behind the glass isn't working."

And there were *a lot* of people staring at me from behind that glass. On any given day, six to a dozen people sat in the control room watching us record. John and Ron, the directors, were always there. Glen Keane, the lead animator, was there most days sketching wildly away, and a handful of other animators, sound engineers and producers, as well as a smattering of Disney execs, would pop in and out.

By turning the lights off in the studio and behind the glass, Howard had created a more stagelike atmosphere for me to work in, and it felt so much better. But he didn't stop there. Instead of stepping back out of the studio, he stayed right there beside me, just as he had done during *Smile*, and he helped me create an image of Ariel's grotto in my mind—a small, dark place at the bottom of the ocean, a twinkling of daylight filtering down from the surface, with her best friend, Flounder, swimming around while she shows off the amazing trinkets and treasures she's collected.

"We just need to get you into the space," Howard whispered. "Not thinking about anything—like you're in a cocoon. Think of yourself working more intimately with the mic. You're in a small, enclosed space. Don't perform. Just talk to Flounder."

I knew exactly what he was going for.

"Make it more intimate." I nodded. "Instead of standing in front of the Lunt-Fontanne trying to sing to 1,500 people."

I just couldn't seem to do it.

"You're not quite relaxed in it yet," he said reassuringly.

"I'm trying." I was starting to get frustrated again—not with him, mind you, but with me.

Then he leaned in a little closer and in the faintest of whispers said, "The amazing thing is . . . everything reads on these mics. I mean every little thing that you do is huge. So a big breath isn't needed. Every little breath you take is enormous. Everything registers. It's like . . . you're litmus paper. So try to work with just the intensity. It's about all that emotion—and *not* letting it out."

"Am I still a little too loud?"

"You're great, but . . . intensity—'What would I give . . .' is better than 'WHAT WOULD I GIVE!' Get in on yourself."

I tried to shake the frustration out through my arms.

"Are you getting tired?" Howard asked.

"No. I'm just trying to make my voice . . . *ughhh.*"

I honestly didn't know what my problem was. I wasn't tired. "Part of Your World" is not a vocally challenging song. I could sing it nonstop without a problem. I just couldn't seem to get the hang of working behind a mic. Howard was right: Every little thing I did, no matter how small, read huge.

All told, I think we spent three or four days during that first week laying down passes of "Part of Your World."

The goal was to get one complete pass to tell the whole story. And thanks to Howard's direction, I was able to give the sound engineers plenty of options to create the version we have now. Honestly, if Howard hadn't turned the lights off and walked me through it line by line, who knows what that song would've sounded like.

And it wasn't just me. Sam Wright, who played Sebastian, was also a Broadway guy. Because Sebastian is like, three inches, tops, and Sam is well over six feet tall, he and Howard came up with a plan to help him get into character. By putting the microphone stand up at full height and then setting it atop a stack of apple crates, Sam would always have to look up really high to deliver his lines—just like Sebastian would've had to do.

Howard knew how to get the best out of everyone he was working with. When he looked at us, he didn't see what we couldn't do; he saw what we needed in order to get us where he wanted us. And then he made it happen.

Ron and John were the same way. When we were recording the dialogue, I would have moments where I would close my eyes and think, *Gosh, I am* really *in the moment here. I am nailing this.* And then Ron or John would push the button from the other side of the glass and say, "That was great, absolutely great. But can we do it again?" And so I would, and I'd think, *Yep. Yep. They were right. This one's even better,* only to hear, "Yeah, that's good. But can we just try it *this* way?" After a while, I'd start to think, *Okay, maybe I don't know what they want.*

In live theatre, you just say it, and it's out there. But with voice-over, it's take after take after take—a little softer, a little louder, a little higher, a little lower, a little breathier, a little faster, a little slower—again and again and again.

Sometimes when nothing I was doing seemed to be working, I'd say, "Why don't you just give me a line reading, and I'll copy it." I wasn't being sarcastic. I'm actually a pretty good imitator, and I let them know right up front that I was perfectly comfortable doing that. Some people aren't; they find the whole idea offensive. But I've never looked at it that way. I'm not worried about "making it my own." My job is to give them what they want. Obviously, they have something very specific in mind, and if I'm not giving it to them, let's just solve the problem and move on.

That's how I came up with the voice for Vanessa, the human Ursula transforms herself into so she can trick Eric. As soon as I learned that this character is basically Ursula borrowing Ariel's voice, I was good to go. I knew I just needed to listen to Pat Carroll's recording sessions and take my cues from her.

For instance, I knew I needed to match her laugh, because it flows from one character to the other in a seamless transition. And Pat has a spectacular laugh—very throaty and robust, which, when she's doing Ursula, turns into this amazing, exaggerated, villainous sort of cackle. So I listened to Pat's lead-in through my headphones, and as soon as she started to laugh, I just mimicked it. We did three or four takes to make sure they could match my pass to hers, and that was it. (Sure, the villain I nailed instantly.) If I'd just tried to wing it, we'd probably still be in the recording studio. I mean, how do you out-Pat Pat?

Occasionally, Ron and John would straight up admit,

"You know what? We're not even sure what we want." I loved that they weren't afraid to admit it because that meant I wasn't necessarily doing anything wrong. Sometimes you just don't know what you want until you hear it. At one point, they even confessed to me that they weren't entirely positive what they were looking for as they listened to the audition tapes. But for some reason, when they heard mine, they said, "That's her! That's Ariel!" And then it took me a year and a half to record the same song I auditioned with.

I also learned that sometimes in animation you don't know what you want until you *see* it.

During the first day of recording, Ron, John, Howard, and Alan gathered everyone around the piano, and we did a complete read/sing through of the script. This, by the way, was one of the innovations Howard brought over from Broadway. Prior to *Mermaid*, all voice-over work was done in isolation by professional voice-over people and then edited to fit. Howard, however, was adamant that the character voices not only be able to do their own acting, but their own singing as well. In other words, he didn't just want voices, he wanted performers—and that's what he got.

Pat, Sam, and I all came straight out of the New York theatre community, as did Rene Auberjonois, who voiced Louis, the chef who almost boils poor Sebastian. And then there was Buddy Hackett. He was one of those larger-than-life personalities who just knew how to take over a room.

Now I'm pretty social. I have no problem walking into a room full of strangers and saying, "Hi, my name's Jodi. I'm so excited to be working with you." But I am not the type to make a grand entrance or command attention. I usually don't sit up front or plant myself next to the VIPs unless I'm told to. I prefer to just sit quietly in the back and listen. Sam and Pat were pretty much the same way.

Buddy, on the other hand, was always "on." He was loud, goofy, and hysterically funny—the perfect choice for Scuttle. He could also be a little . . . *inappropriate*. Whenever we'd run into each other, he'd say something like, "Hey, Ariel—nice tail, kiddo!" And I'd be like, "Buddy, you need to go wash your mouth out with soap," which, I imagine, is exactly what Ariel would say. He was definitely a cutup, though, and utterly unforgettable.

Granted, I noticed that Buddy toned down his jokes when Kenneth Mars, who played King Triton, was within earshot. Ken was a sweetheart, but he was also a really big guy with a huge, booming voice that could be intimidating. In fact, a few times when we were reading lines together, he shouted so loudly at me (as Triton, of course) that I almost cried. Buddy was also a little better behaved around Jason Marin, who played Flounder. Gosh, what a sweet kid. I got to work with him for only one or two days, but he was one of the most gifted 12-year-olds I've ever met. We were definitely an eclectic group.

Anyway, part of Howard's recipe for success was to take all these different personalities and get them together in a room so we could start to hear the characters' voices in our heads and develop some chemistry before we actually got behind the mics.

Since it was the first time any of us had seen the complete script, we didn't know the songs well yet, so Howard and Alan performed all of them for us the first time through, and then we each stepped in to do our lines. After we had gone through the entire script together a couple of times, we broke it down into different scenes, and I did my initial recordings with Ken, Pat, Sam, and Jason. From there, it was all solo work as we fine-tuned everything.

Now at this point, very little had been done in terms of actual animation. All we really had to go by were some rough pencil sketches pinned to a corkboard as a reference point. Everything was still very conceptual. For example, in the early drawings, Ariel was blonde, and Ursula was a much thinner, Cruella de Vil type. The deeper we got into it, though, the more the characters took shape.

That's because the entire time we were recording, the cameras were running—especially in the beginning when we were playing off one another—so the animators could see how we were bringing the characters to life. That's the other reason Howard wanted theatre people as opposed to straight voice-over actors—they're very physical. And animators love that!

Until I worked on *Mermaid*, I didn't realize that most animators are also excellent actors. They have mirrors in front of them, and they'll say the lines as they're sketching so they can see how their bodies and faces change while speaking. But the animators need the voice-over actors to do it first so they know *how* to say the lines. That's why Glen Keane planted himself up there in the control room every time I was recording.

He once told me that in animation, "the voice always comes first." Every character, he said, is "one part vocal cords and five parts attitude." That's why the animators don't really get started until after the recording is underway. The voice—and the spirit behind the voice—is what brings the character to life.

Glen and I met my first day in LA and hit it off immediately. In fact, he gave me one of the nicest compliments I think I've ever received. He told me that he had specifically asked Ron and John to let him illustrate Ariel after watching me record "Part of Your World." Up until then, his real forte had been villains. But he said there was something about the look on my face as I sang that song that reached out and grabbed him. And once it did, he wasn't going to let anyone else draw Ariel but him.

That's not to say he based Ariel 100 percent on me. I'm in there, but Ariel's actually a blend of me; Glen's wife, Linda (who I still think was the inspiration for Ariel's eyes); and Sherri Lynn Stoner. Sherri was the live-action reference model for Ariel. She spent an entire day submerged in an unheated outdoor water tank, wearing nothing but a little bodysuit while the animators sketched her floating hair. They also used her as a reference for water motion, subtle wading movements, and gestures—all the mermaidy stuff, both underwater and on land. They wanted to make sure everything looked real, and Sherri helped them see what Ariel would look like when she was swimming, floating, and sitting on that rock. It's really a fascinating process. Of course, it didn't start with us. Disney had been using live-action reference models since *Snow White*; I think all the princesses have one. It's amazing the lengths Disney Animation goes to so they get it right.

Once the animators had finished their work about a year and a half later, I came back to LA to re-record a handful of lines. Most of it was tiny stuff, like "We've decided to add a sigh here" or "We really love the animation in this scene, but your vocals don't quite match up lip to lip." I think I even re-recorded "Up where they walk, up where they run" because Howard wanted it to punch more.

But there was one line in particular that we all knew needed to be redone—"I love you, Daddy."

Yep, the line at the very end, when King Triton whooshes up out of the sea to give Ariel one last hug and say goodbye after the wedding. I must have recorded that line 50 times the first week I was out in LA and probably another 10 or 20 on my second trip. And still it wasn't quite right. I know you're thinking, *It's only four words, Jodi. How many different ways can you possibly say it?* Apparently, upwards of 70—and all of them wrong.

It wasn't until I saw the scene fully animated with Alan's amazing musical score swelling underneath that I finally got what that moment was all about.

I had been reading it fairly straight, but really it called for a whisper. It's a moment of reconciliation, of saying goodbye without saying goodbye, of acceptance, of Ariel realizing that she's letting go of her old life. It's Ariel asking for forgiveness and letting her father know that no matter what they'd been through, her love for him has always been there. Her respect for him may have wavered back and forth, but her love hasn't. So there's great sorrow, but there's also a sense of relief and gratefulness. She's saying, "I'm sorry," while at the same time realizing and grieving that their restored relationship is now coming to an end. (Please tell me I'm not the only one tearing up right now.) There is just so much packed into those four little words. And I didn't grasp all of it until the scene was fully animated.

So I have a hard time when anyone says that voice-over work is easy or "less than." I have never seen anything more involved, more complicated, or more exacting than feature animation. Such a wide range of personalities, talents, and giftings all come together to create one seamless tapestry. And the only reason it works is because people like Ron, John, Alan, and Howard don't see the limitations of the people around them—they see the possibilities.

When coaching me, Howard didn't see a theatre girl with a huge voice who couldn't work behind a mic; he saw someone he could teach to use her voice in ways she had never tried before. He didn't see a bunch of people who were completely out of their element; he saw a talented group of performers who could help elevate an already amazing art form to new heights. And Ron and John didn't see Howard as a threat to the established way of doing things; they saw him as someone who felt just as deeply about storytelling as they did, as someone they could learn from, and as an innovator who had the potential to put the struggling Disney Animation Studios, which had been moved off the main lot to temporary buildings in Glendale, California, back on the map.

The Little Mermaid succeeded because everyone involved worked toward a common goal, and we complemented each other beautifully. I couldn't have done my job without Glen's help, he couldn't have done his without mine, and Ariel wouldn't be Ariel were it not for poor Sherri shivering away in that giant fish tank to help the animators work their magic. Speaking of which, there were more than 300 artists and animators involved in bringing *The Little Mermaid* to life, not to mention hundreds of sound, production, and visual effects people. Take any one person out of the mix, and *The Little Mermaid* isn't *The Little Mermaid* anymore.

We all have a part to play, and no one person is more important than another. That's one of the things I love most about Ariel: She refuses to see the bad or the "less than" in anyone.

Let's face it: Triton paints a pretty grim picture of humanity, and it's perfectly understandable. The poor guy presumably lost his wife, the mother of his seven mer-girls, to humans. Naturally, he's going to think the worst of people and want to protect his daughters from them at all costs. He's not being cruel when he destroys the grotto; he's just terrified that he's going to lose his little girl. And I think Ariel comes to realize that in the end.

Yet despite everything her father tells her, Ariel can't see how a world that makes such wonderful things could be bad. I think she had probably gone to the surface a lot and been captivated as she watched exciting things happening on the shore, like children playing on the beach and having fun with their families. And of course, she's got Scuttle, who spends all his time flying above, and he doesn't seem to think people are evil. He thinks they're amazing!

Ariel realizes that yes, what happened to her mom was tragic, but that doesn't mean *all* humans are going to hurt her. In fact, she thinks the human world is pretty incredible, and she just wants to see and experience more of it.

It's always struck me as interesting that right before Ariel launches into "Part of Your World," she's kind of wondering out loud, "What's the matter with me? Why am I so weird? Why don't I see the world the way everybody else sees it?"

Frankly, I think the world would be a better and kinder place if more people saw the world the way Ariel does; if they learned to appreciate the beauty in the simple things; if they got to know individuals for themselves instead of just blindly casting judgment or writing them off as "less than." Prince, fish, crab, seagull, sea witch—Ariel doesn't care. She gives everyone a fair shake, and I love that about her.

I love *everything* about that movie. I had no idea back then that it would become such a huge hit. Or that it would launch a new era of Disney Animation. Or that it would still be loved and adored by millions more than 30 years later. None of us did.

Thank goodness we never treated it that way.

15

"Wouldn't You Think I'm the Girl, the Girl Who Has Ev'rything?"

"Now, just remember, when it comes to your singing, you may not like everything you hear."

Okay, so not exactly the congratulatory pep talk I was expecting from Howard as we headed into the theatre on the Disney lot for a private screening of the finished film. But then nothing that had happened that season was quite what I'd expected.

"It's not perfect," he cautioned. "All the notes may not be sung flawlessly. But what we have is perfect for Ariel and the story line."

The funny thing is, I really wasn't worried. When we'd been recording, Ron, John, and Howard all asked if I'd like to come into the control room and listen to the recorded passes, and I'd turned them down. I totally trusted the three of them. Besides, as much of a perfectionist as I was at the time, Howard was 100 times more so. If anyone was going to make sure we got it right, it would be him.

Of course, now *I* was a little freaked out. I don't know why it never occurred to me before, but this was the first time I'd ever watched or listened to myself perform. It just hadn't been an option in live theatre. And now, thanks to Howard's ominous—though I'm sure well-intentioned—greeting, I knew it wasn't going to be perfect.

As Ray and I took our seats alongside other members of the cast and their families, my heart started to race a little. By the time the lights came down, I had both armrests in a vice grip. I wasn't sure whether I was excited or terrified. Either way, I was holding on for dear life.

There was a little bit of static; then Alan's score started playing, and up on the screen three seagulls broke through the clouds, swooping down over a pod of dolphins leaping majestically through the surf. Then, out of the fog . . .

Eric's ship!

Okay, I was excited.

As soon as the ship's crew started singing "Fathoms Below" and poor Grimsby lost his lunch over the rail, it suddenly became real. *Oh, my gosh. I am actually part of a Disney movie. How cool is this?*

A few seconds later, the scene shifted to below the water's surface, the familiar twinkling of the underscore began to swell, and then suddenly there it was:

Walt Disney Pictures Presents

The Little Mermaid

The underwater effect and the little bubbles looked amazing. *I can't believe they hand-painted thousands of those.* Then right in the middle of a school of jellyfish, up popped

With the Voice Talents of

RENE AUBERJONOIS	**BUDDY HACKETT**
CHRISTOPHER DANIEL BARNES	**JASON MARIN**
JODI BENSON	**KENNETH MARS**
PAT CARROLL	**BEN WRIGHT**
PADDI EDWARDS	**SAMUEL E. WRIGHT**

"I didn't realize they were going to do that," I whispered to Ray. I expected that, just like in *Snow White*, *Sleeping Beauty*, and *Cinderella*, these credits would roll at the end, and anyone who really cared could pause the VCR, squint at the names, and try to figure out who's who. Granted, Buddy was probably the only name—and voice—people would recognize, but still . . . I wasn't expecting this.

The shock of seeing my name on the screen was just starting to wear off when . . .

"Flounder, hurry up!"

Oh gosh, there I am.

And then there I wasn't. It was weird: Within minutes of Ariel appearing on the screen, I got so caught up in the story that I completely forgot she was me. The next thing I knew, Ariel was singing "Part of Your World," and I was in tears. Howard was right: It wasn't a perfect pass. But it could not have been *more* perfect for Ariel. Every emotion, every longing, every heartache was laid wonderfully, unmistakably, and imperfectly bare, and it was beautiful—just like he'd said it would be.

A few minutes later, the entire audience applauded at the conclusion of "Under the Sea." (I mean, come on—Sam, the animation, that song—they're incredible!) Everything about watching the film was like being at a Broadway musical, right down to the raucous applause following every song. And it wasn't just during the preview at Disney; it happened at every screening—in more than 20 cities—that I attended throughout the press tour. By the way, the press tour? I hadn't expected that either.

I didn't realize that part of the plan was to show and promote my face to help people connect me and the movie. Disney had never revealed or actively promoted their character voices in the past. But John, Ron, Alan, and Howard had gone full-on Broadway with this one—New York premiere, principal names front and center, postshow meet and greet, photo shoot with *People* magazine—nothing about this was the norm for Disney Animation.

Midway through the press tour, it finally started to click that this wouldn't be a one-and-done, after which I would quietly fade back into obscurity and have to hunt down an old VHS tape at a garage sale someday to prove to my kids I'd actually done it. Nope. As soon as people started connecting the dots, I did too. Ariel was going to be a part of my life for a long, long time. And I certainly hadn't expected that.

Meanwhile, Howard and Alan were already eyebrow-deep in *Beauty and the Beast*. In fact, I remember the day Howard called me to say, "I wanted to be the one to tell you, sweetheart. You're not going to be Belle." Now *that* I totally expected.

"You've just been so visible as Ariel lately, and—"

"Howard, really, it's okay," I assured him. "Honestly, I never expected to be Belle." I really hadn't. Yeah, I had auditioned, but I always assumed it was just a courtesy Disney extended to me in light of how well *Mermaid* was doing. I never in a million years thought I'd actually get it. In fact, for weeks I had been secretly pulling for an old friend of mine, Paige O'Hara.

Paige was also a Broadway girl. We had met years before, back when Ray and I were still dating. Paige was in the touring production of *Oklahoma!* that Ray did the summer I was working in Bermuda. The weekend I flew out to visit him, we all went out to dinner after one of the shows and then sat up talking for hours. I adored Paige instantly. She was sweet, approachable, and so easy to talk to. What I really appreciated, though, was that even though she was a few years older than I was and had been doing professional theatre for a while, she treated me like I was a colleague—not "Ray's little girlfriend who flew in from college." She answered all my questions, gave me a lot of great advice, and shared some really valuable insights. Ours can be a pretty cutthroat industry, so when you find someone as genuine, kind, and encouraging as Paige was (and is), you hold on, and you wish the very best for them in everything they do.

A few days after Howard called, I got a chance to repay that kindness when Paige reached out to me on the eve of her final callback.

"I don't know how to say this," she said, "but . . . well . . . they're kind of asking me to sound more like you."

I almost laughed out loud. In fact, I think I did.

"Are you serious?" How my belching, arm-flailing Ethel Merman impersonation had suddenly become the gold standard, I had no idea. Besides, Paige had a beautiful voice.

"Yeah, they keep telling me to make sure I'm doing this . . . princess storytelling thing, using you as a reference."

Ohhhh . . . Now it all made sense.

"Okay, I totally know what they're talking about. Trust me, sweetie, this has nothing to do with me. It's a Howard thing." And then I passed on everything I had learned from him during our recording sessions—"Just tell the story"; "Don't focus so much on the actual notes"; "Don't worry about sounding pretty and perfect"—the complete Howard Ashman guide to "not singing," from one Broadway belter to another.

"You're going to be great, Paige," I assured her.

"You really think so?"

"Absolutely. You are so perfect for this role."

And darned if she wasn't.

I just love it when good things happen to good people.

And then there's what happened to me. . . .

~~~~~~~

Just as everything was starting to come together for me professionally, everything else in my life started falling apart.

Shortly after *Smile* closed, Ray and I had signed on for an international tour of *Once upon a Mattress*. I followed that almost immediately with a production of *West Side Story* in Venice. Then I did another short-lived Broadway show called *Welcome to the Club*, which my dear friend Frank Rich shut down nine days after it opened. *Gosh . . . that guy.* The one saving grace of that show was that I met Marcia Mitzman, who became my longtime best friend. Thank God for tiny blessings. And in the middle of all of that, I was flying back and forth to LA to record for *Mermaid*.

Ray and I were constantly jumping from show to show, and while I was grateful for the work, it started to take its toll. Emotionally, I was really wearing down. Everything was happening so quickly, and I wasn't making enough time to take care of myself or to focus on growing spiritually. I was able to pull it together for work, put on a happy face, and get the job done, but outside of the spotlight, I was struggling, both in my personal life and in my marriage.

Ray and I barely saw each other, and when we did, I was not in a good headspace. A lot of unresolved stuff related to my parents' divorce and my relationship with my dad began bubbling to the surface.

After the divorce, my dad left and wasn't really a part of my life. I saw him maybe 25, 30 times before he passed away, but because of his own issues (he had bipolar disorder), he was never able to be the father I needed. He didn't attend my wedding or walk me down the aisle. That sense of abandonment was at the root of my struggles.

Granted, I suppose every couple brings some baggage into their marriage with them. But while Ray had brought a little overnight bag, I felt as though I were dragging a steamer trunk, two suitcases, and a garment bag behind me, and I had no idea how to handle it. When Ray and I started dating, I was 18 and, in some ways, searching for security and stability . . . for someone to take care of me the way my dad never had. After Ray and I married, I think Ray took on the role of that missing father figure. As a result, I was torn between being a wife and feeling like a child. The whole situation was a mess.

Instead of drawing Ray in closer and leaning on him for support, I found myself pushing him away and developing some unhealthy relationships outside of our marriage, and eventually Ray did too. We knew we were hurting each other, and we both felt terrible about that. We just didn't know what to do.

Ray was the first and only serious relationship I'd ever had, and we had married so young. My mom did an amazing job of raising me, but because it was mostly just the two of us, I never learned how to navigate the rough patches that come hand in hand with marriage. By the time I realized Ray and I were in trouble, I was already in over my head.

I felt so guilty. I knew Ray deserved better. The problem was, I didn't know how to *be* better. I wasn't even sure I wanted to be married anymore. And that terrified me.

Meanwhile, as Ariel, I was suddenly getting all these wonderful opportunities to talk about my faith, and I could not have felt like more of a hypocrite. Here God had blessed me with an amazing husband and an incredible ministry, and I felt like I was failing both of them miserably.

By the end of 1990, things had gotten so bad that Ray asked me to move out of our apartment so we could take some time apart and get couples counseling. I knew he was right; we did need some space, and I did need to talk to someone. The question was, where was I going to go?

That's when Glen's wife, Linda, said, "Just come here."

"Really, you'd do that?" I was completely taken aback.

Glen, Linda, and I had gotten to be pretty good friends over the past year and a half. I used to pop into Glen's office from time to time to talk and to see how the animation was coming along. He and Linda were both believers, and they'd invited Ray and me to attend their men's and women's Bible studies a few times. We were close enough that they knew Ray and I were having problems. Still, I never expected to be on the receiving end of such a generous offer. That's just the kind of people Glen and Linda are. I didn't even have to ask.

"Of course!" she insisted. "Just grab a suitcase and come stay with us."

So that's what I did. The Keanes even turned their sitting room into a bedroom for me. I tried to stay out of their way as much as possible and help out whenever I could. They had two kids, and I would babysit them on weekends or whenever Glen and Linda wanted a night out. I walked the dogs, looked after the place when they were away—anything to be helpful and show my appreciation. I'm sure having me there was an inconvenience, but they never once made me feel that way.

More importantly, they never made me feel judged or inadequate. And believe me, it wouldn't have taken much. At that point, I was utterly convinced that I had blown my one and only chance to make my marriage work. I felt like a complete failure as a wife and as a Christian. But Glen and Linda never said, "Listen, you've got to stay married or God's never going to forgive you." They weren't like that at all. Instead, they were forever reassuring me that no matter what happened between Ray and me, God would always love me and give me peace about my decision.

"God's not done with you yet," they would tell me. "You're a work in progress, and this is all part of the journey. You're going through a rough patch right now, but God has a plan for you. He loves you, and He's going to get you through this."

Glen and Linda encouraged me to think about who Ray was as a person, what he meant to me, and everything we'd been through. They challenged me to take a step back and ask myself if I really wanted to throw all that away. They were such a great source of comfort and guidance. They knew I was walking down the wrong path and making a lot of bad decisions, but they still loved me, and that meant the world to me.

They were also a wonderful model of what a healthy Christian marriage looks like. Glen and Linda had one of those great stories: They'd met in Paris when they were young, gotten engaged nine days later, and had been together ever since. Oh, they'd had their share of ups and downs—they made sure I knew that. They never tried to pretend. They had issues like everybody else. In the three months I was there, I saw typical family bickering and heard occasional raised voices when one of the kids did something they shouldn't have. But they just had a much healthier perspective on marriage than I did. Whereas I was incredibly idealistic (or fatalistic—take your pick) and perceived every little bump in the road as the beginning of the end, they were incredibly realistic. They knew their marriage was never going to be perfect, but they were committed to doing the hard work of making it work, together.

They also introduced Ray and me to Buster and Gina Holmes, a couple from their small group who did marriage counseling. We saw Buster and Gina together and individually, and though it did help to have an outside perspective, this time was still incredibly difficult. It was just so painful to see Ray hanging on, waiting and worrying, and to be honest, it made me feel like even more of a failure. Sometimes I felt so bad I could barely look at him. I was in such a state of crisis, questioning my value as a wife and as a human being. Seeing all the pain we were causing each other was almost too much to bear. Everything just felt so hopeless.

As I was driving back to Glen and Linda's after a night out, I pulled into a parking lot by a canyon overlook, where I completely broke down, sobbing and screaming. All I could think was, *If I press down on the gas pedal, it will all be over so quickly*. I just wanted it to end—all of it. But as I sat there, hunched over and crying with my forehead pressed against the steering wheel, I felt God saying, *I'm right here. I'm not going anywhere, and we're going to get through this together. You are not a failure. I'm not done with you yet.*

That night marked a turning point for me. I needed to start putting one foot in front of the other and commit myself to doing the hard work I'd been avoiding for far too long. And the first step was getting my own baggage sorted out.

I found a one-bedroom apartment about 15 minutes away from Glen and Linda's place and moved out of their sitting room. They very graciously gave me some furniture, helped me move, and made sure I knew they were always there if I needed them. Of course, I had never even questioned that. In fact, I have no doubt they would have let me stay with them as long as I wanted, but I needed to get my act together, and that meant getting rid of all outside distractions, focusing on taking care of myself, and rekindling my relationship with God.

I'd always had a roommate, first at school and later on tour. Then of course I went straight from that to being married, and eventually I moved into Glen and Linda's house. I'd never lived anyplace by myself, but that's exactly what I needed. I had always been such a people pleaser, constantly worrying about everyone else. Now it was time to focus on me—at least that's what Gina kept telling me.

"You need to stop worrying about saving your marriage," she said. "Let's put that on the back burner for now, take Ray out of the equation, and just focus on you."

Sound familiar? That's because it's almost the exact same thing Juanita had told me to do a few years earlier. Clearly I had a problem taking a long, hard look at Jodi. For some reason, it was just easier for me to think about myself in relation to someone else. But Gina helped me see that before I could figure out who I was in our marriage, I needed to figure out who I was in Christ, baggage and all.

The next several months were all about self-care and working through the insecurities and unresolved abandonment issues I'd been sweeping under the rug since I was little. It was a long, hard, and occasionally painful process, but sometimes a Band-Aid isn't enough. You have to get to the root of things before the real healing can start.

And Ray did his hard work too. He counseled with Buster to work through his own junk and made a commitment to try to save our marriage. I know there were times we both wanted to give up. And we would not have blamed each other if we had. But for whatever reason, God didn't give him a peace about letting go and moving on. So he hung in there, trusting something better was waiting for us on the other side. I can't even begin to express how grateful I am for that.

The hard work lasted almost a year and a half, but we did get back together. We took things slowly, first spending time together as friends and then "dating" for a while. I realized how much I had missed him and how empty my life would be without him. But I also realized that I had a lot to offer as well. For the first time, I'd taken a long, hard look at who I was—and who I wasn't. The girl I found was far from perfect, but she had a good heart and a lot of wonderful qualities. She also had a wonderfully supportive mom, Nana, sister, brother, husband, and circle of friends who loved her—warts and all. And that felt like a good place to start.

I hate that Ray and I had to go through what we did, but it's part of our story. I do believe God is the author of our lives, and I think He wrote that particular chapter in mine for a reason. He used this season to teach me a lot of things I didn't get a chance to learn before I got married—about commitment, trust, brokenness, and healing. He taught me that you can't just sweep your problems under the carpet, because somehow, some way, they're going to come to the surface. And they need to.

God doesn't waste anything. Even the bad stuff happens for a reason, and if we ignore it, we can't learn from it. You might be able to coexist, play the part, and muddle through, but that's not the abundant life God promised us. In order to have a healthy, productive, fruitful life—and marriage—the personal work's got to be done.

It might be a lifelong process, but it doesn't have to be immobilizing. God is a God of second, third, and fourth chances. He's not going to give up on us just because we've momentarily strayed off the beaten path. And He's not going to let our brokenness keep us from doing what He wants us to do.

The timing of our separation wasn't ideal (if there even is such a thing), but it also wasn't a coincidence. It was almost impossible for me to imagine God using me during that season, but He did. He brought me to the highest point of my career at the lowest point of my life, and I think He did so to show me that He can use anybody at any time, in any way, shape, or form. You don't have to be perfect. You don't need to have your act together. I sure didn't. That's what makes God, God. He can take broken, messy people and use them for good. The only way I could ever have truly failed Ray, my marriage, or God was if I had given up. That's the only way any of us can fail.

Now if there had been some magical, Ursula-like contract that said in effect, "Tell you what, Jodi. All the success you're having right now—being recognized as Ariel, *The Little Mermaid* going through the roof, everything finally coming together for you professionally—all that will go away, but your marriage is going to be healthy," would I have signed?

You bet your life I would have—in a heartbeat.

But that wasn't God's plan. It was never one or the other. Being the Little Mermaid didn't create my problems, and it didn't solve them either. Yet the two will forever be inextricably linked—and I thank God for that. Without *Mermaid*, I wouldn't have met Glen and Linda. And if it hadn't been for Glen and Linda leading us to Buster and Gina . . . I don't know that I'd even be here today.

That season wasn't perfect. I didn't always like what I had to hear, face, or do, but it was exactly what needed to happen—for me and for our story. As painful as it was to go through, our separation made our union that much stronger, and the lessons I learned then are a big part of who I am now.

I finally stopped chasing perfection. I stopped swallowing

my feelings. I stopped seeing myself through everybody else's eyes, and I stopped beating myself up over every little flaw. Every emotion, every longing, and every heartache was laid wonderfully, unmistakably, and *imperfectly* bare. And the end result . . . was *beautiful*.

16

"What Would I Pay to Stay Here beside You?"

I don't remember who called me.

It was March 1991. Ray and I were still separated, and I was living in my little apartment in Canyon Country, just outside of Los Angeles. That I know for sure. And I can remember very clearly what the person said.

"Jodi, Howard isn't doing well. We think this might be it. If you want to see him, you need to come now."

I also remember that my very next call was to the airline.

Less than 24 hours later, I was standing outside of Howard's room at St. Vincent's Hospital in Manhattan.

I'd had an inkling he was struggling during *Mermaid*. Nothing was ever discussed publicly, of course, but Ray and I had lost too many close friends and coworkers over the past decade to miss the signs. There was just a distinctive look about the face and the eyes.

On one of my trips out to LA, our script supervisor, Nancy Parent, had graciously offered to let me stay at her house. Nancy and Howard were best friends, so he was staying there too. One morning over breakfast, I couldn't help but notice him taking a very specific combination of pills. My stepbrother, Michael, had been HIV positive, so I knew what the cocktail looked like. I got the sense that Howard wanted to keep it quiet, so I never said a word or let on that I knew. Even so, it just broke my heart. I loved that man so much, and I had prayed so hard for healing for him. And now . . .

I nudged the door to Howard's hospital room open just enough to stick my head in.

Howard's partner, Bill, and I made eye contact, and he smiled and waved me in. I absolutely adored Bill. He was (and is) such an awesome man—so loving, gracious, and kind. Howard could sometimes come across as a bit curt, which a lot of people misinterpreted as harshness, but the Howard Ashman I knew was not gruff. Howard was a genius, and he knew what he wanted. He was a perfectionist and very driven, but he was also one of the most caring people I'd ever known. He was incredibly self-aware and surrounded himself with people who complemented him well—bubbly, effervescent people like Nancy, and teddy bears like Albert Tavares and Bill.

"Howard, Jodi's here." Bill stood up and offered me the chair at Howard's bedside. Then he gave me a hug and quietly took a seat in the corner.

I sat down and gently took Howard's hand in mine. "Hi, sweetie." I barely recognized him. He had lost so much weight, and when he turned his head to face me, it was clear that he had gone blind. What a horrible disease.

We talked for a few minutes. He asked me how I was doing and what I was working on. And of course, he asked about Ray. I kept everything very light and upbeat. I told him that I was living in LA and that I'd been spending a lot of time with Glen and Linda, which he seemed happy to hear. Then I noticed a little cassette player sitting on the tray table next to his bed.

"What are you listening to?"

He reached for the cassette player. "Audition tapes for *Aladdin.*" That man was amazing. *Beauty and the Beast* hadn't even premiered yet, and already he was hard at work on the next one. And I had no doubt it would be brilliant.

"Wanna listen to a few with me?" His voice was barely a whisper. I was trying so hard to keep it together.

"Absolutely."

He hit play, and the voice of a young tenor filled the room. He was singing a song called "Proud of Your Boy." That song was so special to Howard. It is sort of an auto-biographical lyric about his childhood and his relationship with his mom. Unfortunately, it didn't make it into the final cut of the film (thankfully it was reinstated in the Broadway musical), but the lyrics are spectacular. Of course they are.

"This guy's got good vocal quality, don't you think?"

"Yeah," I said as I caressed the back of his hand with my thumb, "he does." We listened to a few more songs, and I could tell he was getting tired. I glanced back at Bill and he nodded at me, letting me know that it was probably time to wrap things up.

"Sweetie, you need to get some rest, so I'm gonna get going, okay?"

"Okay," he said and lowered his head back down on the pillow. He looked so exhausted—nothing like the Howard I remembered, who'd always been so intense, right up there onstage with you, getting it done, making it right.

Nothing about this was right.

"Thanks for coming to see me." He gave my hand a little squeeze.

"Oh, Howard, thank *you*. Thank you so much." I could feel the tears burning in the back of my eyes. I didn't want to start crying and upset him, but I also couldn't leave without telling him how much he meant to me. How much I appreciated everything he'd done for me. I'd thought of literally nothing else during my flight, but now that I was here . . . How do you tell someone, "Thank you for giving me this wonderful, amazing, incredible life" as their own is slipping away?

"Everything I have right now—my career, my relationship with Disney . . . it's all because of you."

He closed his eyes and shook his head. "No, it isn't. You did this. You did the work."

I looked away from Howard for a second to collect myself and noticed Bill had stood up and taken a step toward the bed. He wasn't trying to rush me; I think he just sensed that I was struggling and was trying to show his support without being intrusive. I couldn't even begin to imagine how difficult this had to be for him.

I took a deep breath and leaned in a little closer. "I want you to know that I'm praying for you, sweetie."

Howard had always known about my faith. He knew that

Cindy and I held those little prayer circles just before the curtain went up every night during *Smile*. He never joined us, but he was always very respectful of it. That was something else I appreciated about him. I didn't want to make him uncomfortable, so I kept my prayers to myself that night. But I had been praying from the moment I walked into his room.

You know what, God? This is an amazing man. I don't know if he knows You, but You know him. You've given him amazing talents and gifts, and those gifts have changed the world. I'm still praying for his healing, but if that's not Your ultimate and perfect plan for his life, then I pray that You'll take him with peace and comfort and relieve him of his pain. And God, I know You are here with him now. I pray that he will know it, too, and that he will choose to turn to You.

It was neither elegant nor eloquent, and goodness knows it wasn't perfect. But it was genuine, heartfelt, and real. And that's all that mattered. Howard had taught me that.

I laid his hand back down on the covers, leaned over, kissed him on the forehead, and said, "I love you."

I turned and gave Bill a quick hug, told him I loved him, and kept it together just long enough to get out into the hall. Then I collapsed onto the floor and just started sobbing. A few seconds later, I heard Howard's voice.

"What is that? Who's crying?"

I looked up, and my heart sank. I had forgotten to pull the door closed behind me.

And as usual, I had been too loud.

I immediately put my hands over my mouth and tried to stifle myself, but the sobs just kept coming. I couldn't even stand up. I could see Bill through the crack in the door.

He smiled gently and told Howard, "It's just Jodi. She's a little upset. I'll go talk to her."

I felt terrible.

Within seconds, Bill was crouching down in front of me. "Are you okay?"

No, I wasn't. "I'm so sorry, Bill."

"It's okay, honey."

No. It wasn't. I was supposed to be the one comforting him.

He pulled me into a big bear hug. "I'm so sorry," I whispered. "I didn't mean to upset Howard . . . or you."

"You haven't upset anyone," he reassured me.

"No, I should have moved farther down the hall. I didn't realize . . ." Then I broke down again.

Once again, I was crying in a hallway because of Howard.

I remember Bill once telling me that Howard had come home incredibly upset the night after finally telling me I'd been cast as Doria. He'd said, "I just did the most unprofessional thing you can possibly imagine. I told Jodi she had the part—right in the middle of a callback." When he explained why, Bill thought it was incredibly sweet and kind of funny. Howard, of course, was mortified. He prided himself on being the consummate professional—until I needed him not to be.

That was where it had all started.

And I wasn't ready for it to end.

Bill held me for another minute or so until I finally found my footing and was able to pull myself up off the floor. We said goodbye as we walked back toward the room. He went back in to sit with Howard, and I said one final prayer outside his door, then made my way toward the elevator. I got there just as a group of Disney execs were stepping out. We exchanged a few brief words, and then I left. I looked like a mess, but I didn't care. There's no shame in being upset over losing someone you love. In fact, falling apart might have been one of the most honoring things I could have done for Howard that night. A few days later, Howard was gone. I'm so grateful that I was able to see him one last time, to thank him, and to tell him that he was loved—so very, *very* loved.

I flew back out to New York a month or so later to attend Howard's memorial service, where I said goodbye to my dear friend in the most fitting way I could think of—by singing our song. Alan even accompanied me on the piano. I tried to do the phrasing as excellently as Howard had taught me, but the truth is, I barely got through it.

To this day, every time I sing that song, my mind instantly goes back to that afternoon in the studio, and I swear I can almost feel Howard standing next to me, walking me through it verse by verse, line by line, word by word. In a way, it's almost like he's still here. It's no wonder I love singing it so much.

I didn't get to spend much time with Howard that evening at the hospital. It couldn't have been more than half an hour, but I relished every second of it. When I had gotten the call telling me there wasn't much time left, I didn't know if I'd get to see him. After all, I wasn't family, and this was obviously a very sensitive time. I wasn't even sure if Howard wanted to see me. But he was such an integral part of my life that being 3,000 miles away didn't feel right.

That said, I would have been totally fine if I had gotten to the hospital and Bill had stopped me in the hall and said, "It's just not a good time now." I simply wanted them to know I was there—even if all I'd gotten to do was give Bill a hug and say, "I love you guys. Please tell Howard that I love him and am so thankful for everything he's done for me." That would have been enough.

The visit wasn't about me. It wasn't about what I wanted or my comfort level. It was about them. It was about him. I didn't go there with any agenda other than wanting to be there for my friend, no matter what "being there" looked like.

Grief is hard. It's awkward and it's uncomfortable. We don't want to intrude or, God forbid, make it worse by reacting badly, so more often than not, the temptation is to stay away. And yet the worst thing we can do when someone we love is hurting is to do nothing.

I've learned you don't have to make a grand gesture. A phone call or a text letting someone know you're thinking about them—that you're there if they need anything—is enough. At the end of the day, that's all anybody really wants or needs—to know someone cares. Then you just listen and take your cues from them.

The best lesson I ever got in this came from my dear cousin, Robin Myers. In 2015, Robin tragically lost the youngest of her four daughters, Kylie, to cancer. I was always "Aunt Jodi" to Kylie, whom I adored. On a crisp November day about five years after she passed away, I stopped by Robin's house to check on her. We cozied up under blankets out on her deck, and after some general chitchat, I asked her, "How are you doing?" That's when the floodgates opened.

"You know, Jodi, people say time heals and the longer your child is gone, the easier it gets. But that's just not true. It's actually harder. Every year that Kylie has been gone is more difficult, more painful. I miss her more because she's been gone longer."

I had never thought about it that way before. I'm sure others hadn't either. That's probably why, as the years went by, they broached the subject less and less.

"Do your friends ever talk about Kylie?" I asked her.

"No, not that much," she said, "because they don't want to upset me."

"But *you* like to talk about her."

"Yeah, I do. And I like people to remember her."

"Do you want me to talk about Kylie? Would that make you happy, or would it upset you?"

"Jodi," she said, "I would love it if you would talk about her."

I was so glad I asked. I think we make a lot of assumptions about how people process heartache, and if we assume wrong, we can do more harm than good. Everybody handles tragedy differently. Our job isn't to have to have all the answers; nor is it to try and fix the situation, because we can't. Really, the most helpful and thoughtful thing we can do is to simply ask, "How can I best be your friend right now?"

And that doesn't just apply to the bad times. Every day I look for ways to join God in whatever work He's doing—to rejoice with those who are rejoicing and to weep with those who are weeping. To be light and salt. To encourage. To lift up. To listen for God's voice and to follow His will.

One afternoon when I was folding laundry, I felt prompted to text my daughter, Delaney, who was away at college. So I stopped what I was doing, grabbed my phone, and quickly punched out,

*Hey, sweetie. The Holy Spirit just put you on my mind.
I'm not trying to bother you. I just wanted you to know
that God loves you. He values you. He treasures you. He
thinks you're amazing. And He's got you. You just need
to keep taking one small step at a time and know that
He's going to direct you where you need to be.*

And then I just went back to folding laundry. A few hours
later, when Delaney finally got out of class, she immediately
responded, "Thank you, Mom. That was so sweet. I really
needed that today."

The thing is . . . that text wasn't really from me. It was
God's way of reaching out to one of my kids when they
needed it. I was simply His messenger. And I love that I get
to do that!

It's so amazing to me that God is always thinking of
my kids, even when I'm not. That's how God works. And I
believe God communicates with us whether we know Him
or not.

When people say things like "It's so strange, but when I
woke up this morning, so-and-so was really on my mind," I
believe that's Him. It's not just a coincidence. When somebody suddenly pops into your mind, it's for a reason. And
I think everybody needs to heed those promptings. I really
do. I mean, what does it take? Ten seconds to fire off a quick
text that says, "Hey, I just woke up thinking about you. How
are you?" or "Gosh, I miss you" or "Hey, I hope everything's
okay."

Usually when that kind of thing happens to me, the person ends up texting me back something like "Oh, that's so

After having a boy and a girl, Mom wanted a pony. She got me instead!

Here I am at six, pretending to walk the red carpet

ABOVE
At 12, I was about as close to Carole King as I was ever going to be

LEFT
My last performance at Millikin, playing Polly Peachum in *The Threepenny Opera*

ABOVE
My first Equity job! With Ray on
the *Joseph* national tour in 1982

LEFT
Singing "Tonight" with Ray in
Nashville in the summer of 1980

ABOVE
One of seven parts I played
in my Broadway debut,
Marilyn, in 1983

RIGHT
In Lake Geneva, Wisconsin, on our
wedding day, May 19, 1984

Receiving the keys to the Kingdom from Mickey on the opening night of *Smile*. Ha! Who knew?

Our first Christmas in our tiny New York apartment

Getting ready for my first leading role on Broadway

Trying hard to *Smile* in my dressing room on closing night

I still love working with Alan Menken.
This is from a performance we did
together at the Hollywood Bowl
in 2016

ABOVE
Howard. What would
I pay to have you beside
me again?

RIGHT
Two of my favorite
Disney family members,
Glen Keane (LEFT) and
Roy Disney (RIGHT)

With my amazing directors
John Musker (LEFT) and Ron
Clements (RIGHT) at the
"Happiest Place on Earth"

Harry Groener sweeping me off my feet in *Crazy for You* in '92

Singing "Someone to Watch Over Me" every night . . . so magical!

Ray and I with our dear friend Barry Moss at the 1992 Tony Awards

"Made it!" Graduating from Millikin in 1993

ABOVE LEFT
With Ray in 1994. Still "My One and Only"

ABOVE RIGHT
With my two favorite guys, Ray and McKinley, at our vows renewal, May 21, 1999

LEFT
McKinley's infamous meeting with Tom Hanks at the *Toy Story 2* premiere

Celebrating Christmas with our first family performance in Tampa in 2006

Our first family trip to Disney World—all six of us! (Ray and me; McKinley and his wife, Mackenzie; and Delaney and her boyfriend, Hayes)

ABOVE
Kylie and I riding my favorite Disney attraction, Expedition Everest, in 2014

LEFT
Sharing the concert stage with Delaney in 2022 . . . a dream come true!

Becoming a Disney
Legend in 2011 . . .
what an honor!

ABOVE
My favorite event! Narrating the Candlelight
Processional at Epcot in 2021

LEFT
With my mom; my sister Jill; and my brother
Allan in 2021

This is us
in 2022

funny. I was just about to text you" or "I was thinking about you too!"

I think God wants us to be connected. He wants us to be there for each other. And when we're too busy or too caught up in our own drama to realize it, He reminds us.

I had a lot going on in my life during spring 1991— almost none of it good—but when I found out Howard was in the hospital, there was no way I wasn't going to do something. I didn't have any plans beyond getting on that plane. I didn't have any great words of wisdom to offer. There was nothing I could do to stop what was happening and nothing I could do to make it better, except to make sure that Howard knew how much he was loved. That may be the most extraordinary thing we can do for anyone.

Whenever I spend time with somebody who's important to me, I make sure they know how I feel about them. I don't worry about how it looks or what they might think; I just don't want to leave anything unsaid because life is so fragile and so precious—and it can change in a heartbeat.

I don't know how many times every day I text or tell my kids and my husband, "I love you," but it's a lot. Lately, when the kids are home, I've even taken to walking them to their cars when they go out—even if it's just to go see a friend or go to the store. We do a little hand signal of hearts, we blow kisses, and we wave goodbye. Then I pray over the vehicle, asking God to send angels to protect them and to bring them back home safely.

Sometimes the kids will tell me, "You know, you really don't have to walk me out to the car."

"I know I don't have to," I tell them, "but I like to."

The other night, it was about 32 degrees out, and there I was standing in the driveway in my pajamas, praying over my son's car. Delaney and a few of their friends were with McKinley, and I'm sure I probably looked ridiculous, but I didn't care. They're my kids. I love them, and I want them to know that. In fact, that may be the *one* thing I can't say loudly enough.

17

~~~~~~

"Who Could Ask for Anything More?"

"Listen, I need to ask a huge favor . . . as a friend."

Honestly, I would have done almost anything for Barry Moss. After all, he got me my first professional touring job and—along with it—my Equity card.

"I'm casting a new Gershwin musical called *Crazy for You*, and we've been looking for someone to play the leading lady, Polly Baker, for about a year now. I was wondering if I could fly you out to New York for an audition."

Except that . . .

Ray and I had just started "dating" again, and things were going really well. As much as I would've loved to help Barry out, now was not the time for the two of us to be living 3,000 miles apart. Besides, we both loved Los Angeles, and the thought of going back to New York City and living in those cramped quarters with no car, no beach, and no mountains? No way.

"You know what, Barry? I appreciate it. I really do. I'm just not feeling that right now. Ray and I have been separated for a while, and we're just starting to work on our relationship. So thank you *so* much. But no, thank you."

Barry was quiet for a few seconds. "Tell you what. Let me fly you in so you can audition, and if you get the job, you don't have to take it. How's that?"

Then I went quiet for a few seconds. *What's the point of going all the way out there if I know I'm not going to take it? For that matter, what's the point of them bringing me all the way out there if they know I'm not going to take it?* I figured Barry must have seen everyone else and just wanted to make sure he had ruled out every possible option.

Well, I thought, *it's a free trip to New York. I could stay for a couple days, catch up with some friends, and then come right back.* I did owe Barry a lot. Ray and I both did. He had gotten Ray his start too.

"Okay—as a personal favor. But you need to make it crystal clear to them that I have no intention of moving back to New York. I'm serious, Barry. Even if for some weird reason they actually like me, I'm not doing it."

"Done!"

A few days later, I tossed two days' worth of clothes and my tap shoes into an overnight bag and flew to New York. They put me up in a lovely hotel, and Barry sent over some sheet music so I could familiarize myself with a few of the songs. I had to admit, it was a great list—"I Got Rhythm," "Someone to Watch Over Me," "Embraceable You," "But Not for Me" . . . classic Gershwin.

I'm still not doing it.

When I got to the theatre, Barry was waiting for me along with another old work friend of mine, Susan Stroman. Susan was awesome—sweet, down to earth, and an amazing choreographer. *Barry didn't mention Stro was involved in this show too.* Not that it mattered. I still wasn't doing it.

It was one of the easiest auditions I'd ever done. Don't get me wrong; it wasn't like I phoned it in or anything. I still gave it my best effort. But knowing it wasn't going to happen—and I was perfectly okay with that—took all the pressure off. I sang a few measures of "I Got Rhythm" and "Someone to Watch Over Me." Then they handed me two or three pages of the script, gave me a few minutes to rehearse it backstage, and had me run through some dialogue with a reader. And that was it.

"Thanks, Jodi. That was great." I didn't recognize the voice. I knew there were several people out in the house watching, but Barry and Susan were the only two I knew personally.

I shaded my eyes from the lights. "Will there be a dance call? I brought my tap shoes with me."

"No, I don't need to see you dance. I know what you can do." That was Susan. And yeah, she did. But still . . . *They did fly me all the way out here.*

"Oh, okay." I turned to walk offstage, then stopped. "Are you sure you don't want me to just do something for you while I'm here?"

"Nope," came the voice from the darkness. "We're good." *That's weird.*

"Okay. Well . . . thank you." And with that I smiled, waved goodbye to Barry and Susan, and quietly walked off the stage. *I am so not getting this.*

No sooner did I get back to my hotel room than the phone rang. It was Susan.

Yep. I got it.

"What's wrong? Why don't you sound happy?" Susan was such a lovely person. I hated to let her down.

"Well, it's just that I told Barry . . ." Then I ran down the list: "Ray and I are living in LA . . . We're just getting back together . . . I'm working with Disney . . . Really trying to focus on the voice-over thing right now . . . I just don't think New York . . . Or doing eight shows a week . . ."

She heard me out, then said, "Okay, well, you don't have to make the decision right now. Take a few days. Think about it. Then give us a call."

"Okay. Thanks, Stro."

"Oh, and Jodi?"

"Yeah?"

"Congratulations."

I'm still not doing it.

The next few weeks were rough. Ray and I went back and forth endlessly trying to decide what to do. We were not only deciding about the job but also about how to proceed with our relationship after almost 18 months of being separated. I didn't even have a theatrical agent anymore. Since I had been focusing primarily on voice-over work with Disney and Hanna-Barbera at that point, it just didn't make sense. Ray, however, seemed far less concerned about that than I was. He had seen enough contracts in his day to take over should the need arise. He even had a plan to get us out of the deal completely: "Whatever they offer, we'll just turn it down." Made sense to me. And it worked. Until they called back with an offer unlike anything either of us had ever seen before.

"We can turn this down. Honestly, Ray, it's not worth it. I'd rather stay here and focus on us."

Ray looked at me for a minute, then said, "I think you should go."

What?

"We're stronger now. We can handle it."

"You're kidding, right?" He had to be. "We just got back together. My taking off now feels like the worst decision we could possibly make."

"What if I come with you?"

I hadn't considered that. "Do you really want to go back to New York?"

"Well," he conceded, "not to that apartment. If we did do it, we'd need to find a bigger place."

I was stunned. He was actually considering it. Even weirder, so was I.

Ray was right. We were a lot stronger now as a couple than we were a year and a half before. *And if he came with me . . .*

"Jodi, you don't have to take it. I'm just saying that if you do, you wouldn't have to go by yourself. We would do it together."

I still wasn't convinced.

"You know what . . . let's give it to God. Let's stop talking about it, put it in His hands, and see what happens."

Here's what happened: They sent me the script.

"Well, what do you think?" he asked.

"Honestly, Ray, I don't know if this show is gonna run for six weeks or six months." But look at my track record: *Marilyn* ran for two weeks and *Smile* for six, and *Welcome to the Club* barely made it over one. Granted, I did love the songs. And it sounded like they were planning to do the out-of-town tryout in Washington, DC, which is a great city. Susan was involved. So was Barry. And it was a phenomenal cast.

So what are we talking about here? A month of rehearsals, maybe a month in DC, another week or two of previews, then maybe a month before Frank Rich shuts us down? Odds are we'll be back in LA in five months.

Ray and I had both been praying for some sense of peace about it for days, and much to my surprise, the answer was starting to feel like a yes.

I set the script down, sighed, and looked over at Ray. "Wanna pack a couple of suitcases, see if we can find a nice sublet, and call it a day?"

Yep. We were doing it. We decided to move back to New York together, with a solid commitment to our marriage. Ray stepped in as my agent and my manager. We were a strong team, both personally and professionally.

I signed a one-year contract, and Ray arranged for us to sublet a friend's apartment on 75th Street and Broadway. It was a beautiful building in a great neighborhood, just a quick subway ride to the Shubert Theatre, where I'd be performing.

From day one, it was clear that this experience was going to be totally different from my previous shows. Everything was so much more peaceful and organized, and it felt solid and relaxed. There was none of the stress and the tension we felt during *Smile*. A lot of that was because we had two great producers in Roger Horchow and Elizabeth Williams. Both were incredibly kind and very supportive of the cast, and they never stepped out of line, tried to force their opinions on anyone, or offered input unless asked. They never spoke directly to the cast about their ideas but instead ran everything through our director, Mike Ockrent, and Susan.

Part of the problem with *Smile* and *Marilyn* was that there were far too many cooks in the kitchen, with a wide variety of backgrounds. Yet they all chimed in at will, contradicting each other, confusing the cast, and muddying the waters. But *Crazy for You* was run exactly how a Broadway show should be run—calmly, collaboratively, and professionally.

The best part was, without all the constant bickering and changes to the script and choreography, we had plenty of time to focus on the fun part—developing our characters. And did I have a great character in Polly.

The show was based on the 1930 Gershwin musical *Girl Crazy*, and Polly was a combination of the characters played by Ginger Rogers and, of all people, Ethel Merman. How's that for irony? Polly, the only female in an all-male Western town, is caring for her dad after her mother passed away. She falls in love with a young banker who sweeps in to foreclose her father's theatre. Polly is kind of an all-American girl—fiery, tenacious, and independent. To be honest, she reminds me a lot of Ariel.

And of course, I got to sing all those incredible songs— especially "Someone to Watch Over Me." It's such a beautiful ballad, and Polly gets to sing it all alone on center stage. I used to dream about something like this when I was a kid, standing in front of the bathroom mirror while singing into the end of a hairbrush. I would just lose myself in that song.

At the end of the first act, there was an epic eight-minute-long showstopper, "I Got Rhythm," which Ethel Merman made famous. Susan's choreography for that number was flat-out unbelievable, and I got to let loose and belt my heart out. The whole thing was just a fantastically joyous experience.

Thank God I decided to do it.

Oh, and the icing on the cake? Frank Rich *loved* it! He gave us a positively glowing review. *Finally.* And you know what that meant—*this* show was gonna run for a while!

Ray and I were doing beautifully. He was there for most of the rehearsals and most of the out-of-town tryout. When his own work took him out on the road, I would use my day off to fly to wherever he was, even if it was only for an afternoon. We were committed to making sure we never went more than a week or two without seeing each other.

It's funny; when we first got married, I thought that if Ray and I were truly meant to be together, we wouldn't have to work at it. It would just happen. Wow, was I wrong. You do need to work at it. Not only that, you should want to work at it. You should want to put the work in on anything that's of value to you.

Just because Barry and the rest of the team said "I do" at my audition didn't mean I could just coast the rest of the way. I still had a lot of work to do. But I was committed to it, and because the show and so many of the people involved in it were important to me, I enjoyed every moment. I know it sounds like a cliché, but you really do get out of something what you put into it. Before our separation, there were times I was nowhere near as invested in our marriage as Ray was. Making it work just felt too hard. He'd been trying to pull me along, and I'd been tugging the other way. You can't move forward like that. But now we were in lockstep, and the difference was night and day.

After the show opened, we fell into a comfortable routine. It usually took me a good two to three hours to unwind after a performance, so whenever he was in town, Ray would have dinner waiting for me when I got home, and we'd sit and talk. We had both grown so much since the separation, and we'd developed a much greater appreciation for what each of us brought to the relationship.

Before we split up, I thought that in order to be a successful couple, we had to agree on everything (What can I say? I was young), and the fact that Ray and I have wildly different temperaments didn't help. I'm more of a fly-by-the-seat-of-your-pants type of person, while Ray tends to be more analytical. When something upsetting happens, I tend to get past it pretty quickly, whereas Ray usually takes a couple of days to process things. Also, one of Ray's superpowers is his ability to see both sides of a situation almost immediately, and I used to find that so annoying. I just wanted him to see *my* side, period. And wow, had that made for some lively sessions when we were being counseled by Buster and Gina.

But just because we processed things differently didn't mean we couldn't work together as a couple. In fact, we realized that our differences complemented one another beautifully. A lot of my weaknesses were Ray's strengths, and vice versa, which actually made us a fantastic team. And even though we were wired differently, we had the same goal—a strong, loving, Christ-centered marriage—and this time, we were both committed to making it work.

That's what made *Crazy for You* so successful as well. Everyone brought different strengths and weaknesses to the table, but we were equally committed to working hard as a team toward the same goal, with no egos, no dissension, and

no power struggles. The result was one of the most spectacular shows on Broadway that year.

In fact, just three months after we opened, the Tony nominations came out, and *Crazy for You* received nine of them,
including Best Musical, Best Choreography, Best Direction,
Best Actor, and, yep, Best Actress. Talk about blessings on
top of blessings.

The whole month leading up to the awards ceremony was
a fantastic experience for me, in part because I knew I wasn't
going to win. That's not false modesty on my part. From the
moment the nominations were announced, everybody knew
that honor would go to Faith Prince from *Guys and Dolls*.
Faith was an icon in the industry and super talented, but she
had yet to win a Tony. This, however, was clearly Faith's year.
We all knew it, and everyone, myself included, was thrilled for
her. Truth be told, I was far more interested in winning Best
Musical. We were up against some amazing shows, so unlike
my category, that one would be a real nail-biter. Even so, all
I had to do was relax and enjoy myself. There was no pressure, no nerves, no expectations—just a wonderful week of
brunches, lunches, and get-togethers with the other nominees.

The Tonys aren't like the Academy Awards. The whole
event reminds me of a big family reunion. The Broadway
theatre community is pretty tight—at least it was back in the
nineties—so we all pretty much knew everybody else. But
because we were all working the same eight-shows-a-week
schedule, we didn't always get a chance to see each other's
work. That's the other thing that distinguishes the Tonys
from other award ceremonies: It's kind of a mini Broadway
show in itself, packed to the hilt with live performances.

That year, our cast was invited to perform the opening

number. It was a four-minute medley of "I Can't Be Bothered Now," "Slap That Bass," "Shall We Dance?" and "I Got Rhythm" that not only pulled in most of the cast but also beautifully highlighted Susan's choreography. And there is nothing like performing in a theatre filled with your peers, because Broadway people are so appreciative of everything that goes into it. Plus it was like getting a four-minute commercial for the show, and we didn't have to pay for it. That's huge. I mean, it's not like you can just go down to the local Cineplex if you want to see a Broadway show. You have to come to New York. That's quite an investment, so to be able to show a national audience, "Hey, look what you're missing," can do wonders for ticket sales.

The whole evening was magical. Susan deservedly won for Best Choreography, and William Ivey Long won for Best Costume Design. Of course, to no one's surprise, Faith won Best Actress, and hand on heart, I could not have been happier for her. The highlight of the evening, however, was when *Crazy for You* won Best Musical. That was such a win for all of us. It was not only a validation of all the hard work everyone had done over the past year but also meant we would get to enjoy performing it for months, possibly years, to come. That's what happens when everyone pulls together and gives their very best.

I honestly don't remember many details about that evening aside from the joy of performing in front of my theatre family, celebrating Susan's success, and watching Roger and Elizabeth marvel speechlessly at the Best Musical statuette. That's what musical theatre is—pure emotion—and I just wanted to savor every second of it.

Ray and I had been talking for a few months about moving back to LA and starting a family as soon as the show finished its run, so I knew this was going to be my last hurrah—on Broadway anyway. And what a way to go out—with the leading role in a Tony Award–winning musical. Gosh, I loved that show. I loved going to work every day and seeing my name up on that marquee. I loved going out there and singing my heart out every night. I love that God saw all of this coming when I couldn't. Even though I probably didn't deserve it, I love that He loved me enough to let it happen anyway. And I loved Ray to the moon and back. Honestly, who could ask for anything more?

18

"But Not for Me"

Not long ago, someone asked me what I had on my bucket list. And you know, I really struggled to come up with an answer. Obviously, I'm looking forward to becoming a grandmother someday, and I'd like to think Ray and I still have a few grand adventures ahead of us, but for the most part, I'm content to follow the Lord wherever He chooses to take me. After all, His plans for me are always going to be infinitely better than anything I could come up with. All I really care about is running the race well, and when I get to the end, knowing I did everything I could to love and serve others well and use my gifts and talents to the best of my ability.

When my moment comes to stand before God and He asks me, "How were you the hands and feet of Jesus?" and

"What did you do with the gifts I gave you?" I want to be able to answer both questions well. I don't want to have any regrets. I don't ever want to look back and say, "Oh gee, I wish I had done this or that." I want to leave it all out on the stage, completely used up—nothing wasted. That's the way I try to approach everything in my life, because you never know what might come of even the tiniest effort.

I remember way back when I auditioned for *Marilyn*, there were about 20 or so of us standing onstage, and we each had a little number pinned to our leotards. We had just finished a dance call, and the casting team called out the numbers of the girls they wanted to stay. If your number wasn't called, that was it—you were cut.

Well, I thought I'd had a pretty solid audition all the way through. There were just a lot of unspoken signals, like heads bobbing up and down whenever I was singing and my almost always being placed in the front row during the dance calls—that kind of thing. In fact, I distinctly remember standing there thinking, *I have so got this.* But then my number didn't get called. For the life of me, I could not figure out what I'd done wrong or what more I could have done. And for some reason, I just couldn't let it go.

So I grabbed my stuff, but instead of leaving straightaway, I went down into the house and approached Barry, my casting-director friend, who had gotten me the audition in the first place. By the way, how I summoned up the nerve to do that at the ripe old age of 20, I have no idea. I wasn't rude or argumentative; I just said, "Hey, Barry, I wanted to thank you again for getting me this opportunity. I'm just a little—" *How do I want to put this?*—"I just *really* thought I did well."

Barry looked completely baffled. "What are you talking about?"

"It's just that my number didn't get called, and I thought—"

"Jodi," he interrupted, "we *did* call your number."

"No, you didn't."

"Yes, we did."

"No, you didn't."

Well, Barry immediately started riffling through the stack of photos and résumés with the numbers attached, and that's when he noticed that mine had fallen on the floor. Now, I have no idea what would have happened if I had just left—if Barry would have eventually called me back or if they would have figured, *Well, guess she doesn't want it*, and moved on to someone else, but from that moment on, no matter what happened at an audition, I made a point of personally thanking the entire casting team before I left. You just never know, and I'd rather risk looking a little foolish than miss out on a great opportunity.

Granted, stopping to check in with Barry took all of two seconds. Sometimes finishing well takes a little more effort.

Shortly before Ray and I left for New York, I was over at the Disney lot taking care of some business, and I stopped in to say hi to my friend Roy Disney. Roy was the nephew of the late Walt Disney and the chairman of Walt Disney Feature Animation. He had this amazing office inside the sorcerer's hat, and I would pop in and see him whenever I was there.

We were sitting in his office chitchatting—I was telling him how much I loved doing *Mermaid* meet and greets, where I got to talk with kids all over the world—and the next thing I knew, I went full-blown confessional on the poor guy. "I feel like such a hypocrite," I said.

"Why's that?"

God bless Roy. I'm sure he had much more important things to do that day than talk to me, but he never made me feel rushed, unheard, or uncared for.

"I've been leading all these master classes for high school and college students, and it just feels weird because I dropped out of college before I got my degree."

"Well . . . can't you get your degree?"

Why was I always so blind to the obvious?

"I don't know. I've never really thought about it."

"Maybe you should. At this stage of your career, you probably don't need it anymore, but if it helps you feel better when you're out talking with kids, wouldn't it be worth it?"

Huh. You see? That's why Roy worked in the sorcerer's hat.

A few months later, I was still thinking about it. *What if I did decide to go back and finish my degree? What would that even look like?*

If anyone would know, it would be Ray. He had gone through the same thing with his university. He dropped out just three quarters shy of earning his degree to start working professionally and help support his parents. Ray's situation was a little more complicated, though, because he'd switched majors from pre-vet to theatre midway through, so he lost a bunch of credits. Unfortunately, the university wasn't open to making the concessions he would have needed to make it doable. And after he hit a brick wall, I figured the same thing would probably happen to me.

"You never know," Ray cautioned. "Millikin's much smaller, and it's private. The rules might be different. Plus you still have a lot of people there who know you."

That was true. Steve, my voice teacher, was still there, as was my former acting professor, Terry Williams.

"Not to mention, you're doing a Broadway show right now. That'd be a big win for them. You've got nothing to lose by checking it out."

So I did. It turned out that all I needed to move forward was a unanimous vote from the board of directors, but wouldn't you know it—there was one person who said no. Apparently there had been enough changes to the catalog in the 10 years I'd been out to cause the same problem Ray ran into. So when I asked to pick up right where I'd left off, they thought I was asking for a pass on a bunch of credits. In other words, a free degree.

That's when Steve went to bat for me. He said, "Listen, she had a 4.0. She was a very diligent student. She took a full course load every semester in addition to performing in every show we did her freshman and sophomore years. She's currently in a Broadway show, and she's not looking for a handout. She's willing to do the work."

Steve's speech was enough to turn that one no into a yes. Now I just had to figure out how to do it.

The first thing I did was switch from a BFA in musical theatre to a BA in theatre. Roy was right; at this point my concentration really didn't matter, and making the switch would save me worlds of time. Now all I had to do was cram two years' worth of coursework—a lot of it performance based—into one semester. So . . . wow.

Fortunately, the university had an idea. Since I was

working in my chosen field, they flew four people out to New York to watch my performance in *Crazy for You* and evaluate whether I had mastered enough skills to meet the requirements of my remaining theatre courses. I'm not sure which night they were there, but I must have been "on" because I passed with flying colors.

That left just two general-ed courses, which, thankfully, I could do remotely from New York. Most evenings, I'd work on my papers for a few hours after I got home from the theatre. I was usually pretty wired after a show anyway. Why not put that energy to good use?

I used my one week of vacation time that year to fly back to Illinois and take all my practical final exams on campus. It felt great to be back, and I got to close out the week by leading a master class and giving a solo concert performance. A few weeks later, I flew back out on my day off to graduate and walk with the rest of the class. It was absolutely wonderful. Ray was there, and my mom, sister, and Nana all drove down to watch and celebrate with me. Roy Disney even sent me a card and a little gift.

As good as it felt to finally graduate, it was never really about getting that piece of paper; it was about the sense of accomplishment. I was a good student, and I did want to finish what I had started. I also wanted to be able to look into the eyes of the theatre students I was working with and say, "You can do hard things. If I can do it, you can do it." I didn't want to be insincere. I wanted to really mean it.

That was a wild season because I was also going into the studio a few afternoons a week to record *The Little Mermaid* animated TV series. But somehow we made it work, and do you know what? The man in the magic hat was right: It was worth it. It's always worth it when you go that extra mile. It's even better when you go that extra mile for someone else.

~~~~~~~~

When I came back to Broadway to do *Crazy for You*, it was with a much different mindset than I'd had when I was working on *Smile*. I think it was a combination of maturity from having been in the industry for a while, not feeling as though I constantly had to prove myself, and a shift in priorities. I had just turned 30, and as the female lead, I wanted to connect with the cast—to create a sense of family, and to really love them well.

When I left the apartment each afternoon, I would say, "Hey, God, I'm ready to join You in Your work today. Don't know what that looks like, but if You'll just put somebody on my mind or on my heart, I'll follow Your lead from there."

I would usually get to the theatre around 5:00 and take my time warming up; then I'd try to make the rounds to several of the dressing rooms and check in to see how everyone was doing.

After that I'd head over to the girls' ensemble dressing room. I loved going around straightening up the makeup stations, and sometimes I'd leave a few of the girls encouraging notes—just something to let them know I was thinking about them.

And then as I'd done with *Smile*, I would organize a quick prayer circle with whoever wanted or needed it five minutes before "Places" was called.

But the preshow check-ins were where I felt the most useful—especially when it came to talking with some of the young parents in our show. I could see there was a real struggle for actors trying to balance being a Broadway performer with being a present, involved parent, and at times, it was heartbreaking to watch.

I think there's this misguided assumption that Broadway performers have the world on a string, but really, acting is a job like anything else—a really challenging one that takes place predominantly during dinnertime, homework time, bath time, and bedtime. You work eight shows a week, usually with only one night off, and every weekend is booked. That means if you've got a school-age child, you're down to just one or two waking hours a day with them, sometimes for months at a time.

I can't speak for today, but back in the nineties, most of the theatre community lived outside Manhattan and commuted in, which meant they had to be out the door before their families sat down for supper and often didn't get home until midnight or later. And of course every Saturday they missed T-ball games, dance classes, birthday parties, trips to the zoo, and all the other fun activities families do together on the weekends. And it wasn't just the moms. I saw plenty of dads affected by it too.

I loved performing on Broadway. I really did. And *Crazy for You* certainly would have opened a lot of doors for me moving forward. But I also wanted to have a family and be with my children more than a Broadway show schedule would allow. Seeing the challenges some of my castmates were dealing with trying to be there for their kids while doing eight shows a week was all the confirmation I needed—being a mom on Broadway was definitely not for me.

Fortunately, God had blessed me with a wonderful voice-over career. It might not have been as glitzy or glamorous as

Broadway, but I could just zip into the studio with a baby in my arms, do my thing, and still be home in plenty of time to burn dinner.

I also knew that although there were plenty of recording studios in New York, raising a family in Manhattan wasn't for me either.

One of my closest friends at the time lived on the Upper East Side, and she had three kids, all under five. One day I watched her trying to maneuver a double stroller along a crowded sidewalk as she tried to wrangle her third child, who was wandering next to, in front of, and behind her, and I just thought, *Wow . . . she's amazing, but I don't think I'm cut out for that.*

Sidewalk gymnastics aside, Ray and I both knew we didn't want to raise our kids in a small Manhattan apartment, nor did we want to move to Connecticut or New Jersey and have to commute back and forth. We both loved living in LA, and we wanted to find a cozy little home there in the suburbs with a backyard and maybe a playground or park nearby. That was what we both grew up with, and we wanted our kids to have the same experience. So as soon as *Crazy for You* wrapped, that's exactly what we planned to do.

In the meantime, I was going to savor every last second of my time on Broadway, however long that might be. And unlike *Marilyn* and *Smile*, I didn't worry about *Crazy for You* coming to an end because I knew I had something just as good, if not better, waiting for me when it did.

And it did end—at least for me.

Though the show would continue to run for another two years, I did my last performance as Polly Baker on March 13, 1994. It was a happy-sad night. On the one hand, I loved that show. I loved being Polly, I loved our cast, and I hated to see it all come to an end. And yet I couldn't help but feel incredibly grateful. It had been a great run. I'd been there worlds longer than I ever expected, I'd accomplished a lot, and I'd made some great friends. But now it was time to move on—not just from *Crazy for You* but also from Broadway.

God had blessed me with the opportunity to perform in four different Broadway shows, and I can honestly say, I left nothing on the table with any of them. Things didn't always turn out the way I'd hoped or expected, but I had no complaints and no regrets—just a lot of memories of wonderful experiences with wonderful people, many of whom are still in my life today. My only hope was that I'd been able to pour as much love and joy into their lives as they'd poured into mine, and if this was it for me and Broadway, I was good with that.

Not long after I stepped away from *Crazy for You*, Ray and I got a call from our friend Danny Pelzig. We had known Danny for years. He was the choreographer for a few projects that Ray and I had been involved with, and now he was working on, of all things, another Gershwin musical called *My One and Only*. They were getting ready to launch a six-month international tour of cities throughout Austria and Germany, and they had only one small problem: They still hadn't cast the romantic leads. Since Danny knew both of us and I had just finished doing a Gershwin show . . .

"I'm not sure what you guys have going on right now," he hedged, "but is there any chance you two might be interested in playing opposite each other?"

Oh, my gosh. Was he kidding? Ray and I hadn't worked together since that touring company of *Joseph* back in '82.

Neither of us had anything on our schedules, short of moving back to LA and finding a place to live, and the thought of getting to spend six months touring and exploring Europe together before settling down to start a family sounded like heaven.

I think we discussed it for all of 28 seconds. And wouldn't you know, it turned out there *was* something on my bucket list.

We'd never had a honeymoon.

19

~~~~~~~~~~~~~~~~~~~~~~~~~~~~~~~~~~~~~~~

"Someone to Watch Over Me"

There's nothing like the thrill of doing live theatre.

The rush of adrenaline when the stage manager calls "Places."

The warmth of the spotlight on your face.

The telltale twinge in the pit of your stomach seconds before you frantically dart offstage to throw up.

Let me rephrase that: There's nothing like the thrill of doing live theatre . . . while battling morning sickness.

Welcome to 1998. Ray and I had both been cast in another touring production of *Joseph and the Amazing Technicolor Dreamcoat*, and we were super excited about it—that is, until we found out I was pregnant two days before we were supposed to fly out to New York to start rehearsal.

It's not that we weren't excited about this pregnancy.

On the contrary. We were thrilled! Sadly, a few months earlier, we had miscarried our first child when I was six and a half weeks along. That was devastating enough, but now I had a history, and that, combined with my age, put me in the high-risk category. And if Ray and I were doing the math right, the tour was going to stretch all the way up to my sixth month. So . . . yeah.

As soon as we found out, we reached out to the *Joseph* team to let them know what was happening, and to our surprise, they could not have been more supportive. The director pointed out that my role as the narrator was a very maternal one to begin with (bonus points for method acting), and the costume designer offered to modify my wardrobe so my outfits would be looser fitting and easily expandable as I, well, expanded. In short, they weren't the least bit concerned.

"So what do you think?" I asked Ray.

"Well, we'll be together, which is good. And we'll be sitting in big cities close to family and with easy access to doctors and hospitals. It's not like we'd be traveling every day, so there'd be plenty of time for you to rest."

"That's true," I agreed. "And it's not a very strenuous role. The choreography is minimal. It's mostly vocals." And he was right; we *would* be together. That was huge. The only downside was the morning sickness.

And the afternoon sickness.

And the evening sickness.

Seriously. It was incessant—anywhere from 4 to 10 times a day for 17 straight weeks. And can I just say . . . God bless our cast and crew. They kept trash cans for me at either side of the stage and made sure I always had plenty of plastic bags on hand. Our dear friends and castmates Lisa and Eric took every opportunity to keep me laughing onstage and off, and everybody became very adept at getting out of the way when they saw me coming.

The mouthwash and the pizza were my ideas. Don't ask me why, but for some reason, a big, greasy slice of pizza was the only thing that would help calm my stomach. That, or bacon and eggs, and frankly, it was a lot easier to pick up the phone and give Pizza Hut a call an hour or so before curtain every night. Between the pizza and the trash cans . . . let's just say it was fragrant backstage.

But you know what? I never missed a single entrance. I just sat very quietly with my head between my knees, breathing deeply, sipping ginger ale, and doing everything I could to make sure I could get back out there on cue.

~~~~~~

For the most part, the entire tour went smoothly, with the exception of one scary moment when we were still in rehearsal. I was in my sixth or seventh week, and I started bleeding unexpectedly, which was exactly what had happened when I'd miscarried less than a year earlier. Fortunately, we were still in New York, where one of my dearest friends, Kathy Gable, was a pediatric nurse. Panicking, I gave her a call, and she got me in to see her ob-gyn right away.

I was utterly convinced I had lost another baby. I remember Kathy holding my hand during the ultrasound while I just sobbed, waiting for the doctor to break the bad news. *I can't believe this is happening again. Maybe I'm not supposed to be a mom after all.*

Then came words I hadn't expected: "I'm picking up a strong heartbeat."

"Are you serious?" I lifted my head to get a better look at the monitor.

"Yep. Looks like you've got yourself a little fighter here."

I laid my head back down on the pillow and dissolved into tears. *Thank You, God. Thank You so very, very much.*

"Just take it easy," the doctor said, making one final sweep with the wand. "Don't overdo it, and you should both be fine."

"You're sure? I *have* been throwing up a lot."

She just waved me off. "Oh, throwing up's a great sign."

Now there's something you don't hear very often.

But that was it. The rest of the tour went fairly smoothly. I did experience a little more bleeding while we were in Montreal, but once again, the doctor said it was nothing to worry about. I even managed to fly out to Barcelona on one of my days off to do a corporate event for Disney. Because nothing says "Take it easy" like a quick overnighter to Spain.

At one point during the tour, I made an appointment to see my own ob-gyn, Dr. Margolin, in LA. I loved that guy. He was so kind, calming, and reassuring—everything a first-time mom could hope for. Given my history and the slight scare we'd had early on, he decided to run a full battery of tests, just to be safe. When Ray and I went back a few days later for the results, we had only one request: "If you know the sex, please don't tell us. We don't want to know." But as soon as I saw Dr. Margolin's face, I knew something was wrong.

"Ray, Jodi, I'm afraid the baby shows three of the five markers for Down syndrome."

What? I felt as though I'd just had the wind knocked out of me. Ray reached over and grabbed my hand, his own shocked expression a perfect reflection of my own.

"Now, I can't tell you 100 percent that this is accurate," he cautioned, "but based on these results, there is a strong possibility."

Ray and I just sat there, dumbfounded. I was afraid to look at Ray for fear I'd burst into tears. Dr. Margolin had a folder full of test results in front of him, but not one of those tests could answer the question I was most worried about.

I had met countless children with special needs through my Disney events. Many were on the autism spectrum and unable to speak. Others were in wheelchairs. And they just loved and connected with Ariel so much because, like them, she longed for something outside of her own world. And those kids were amazing! Every one of them. So were their parents. But what if those moms had something I didn't? What if I couldn't do it?

"Of course, if you'd like, we can do an amniocentesis to see if we can find some more definitive answers."

I was shaking my head before he finished the sentence, and to his credit, he didn't push it. Dr. Margolin knew where Ray and I were at with our faith. Regardless of what the test results showed, there was no way we were going to terminate the pregnancy; nor would it change the way we felt about our child. Besides, I knew there were risks involved in amniocentesis, and I wasn't willing to further jeopardize our baby's health with a procedure that wasn't going to change our minds or hearts one bit.

Then, through the fog, I heard Ray's voice.

"Thank you, doctor, but we're going to pass on the amnio. All that matters to us is that the baby is healthy. We're going to trust God and pray." He squeezed my hand. "Right?"

I looked at him through tears. "Right."

The next four months were some of the longest and hardest of my life. Ray and I read everything we could get our hands on about Down syndrome so that we could be as prepared as possible, all the while praying for a safe delivery and a strong, healthy baby.

After the production ended, we moved back home to LA, where Ray did his best to keep my spirits up and my mind occupied. That was no easy task once the doctor put me on full bed rest for the final two and a half months. I was allowed to sit up, eat, and go to the restroom, but that was about it. Ray had his agent take him off the market so he could be home with me, and any time he had to leave the house, even if it was just to run to the store, he had a friend come over to sit with me, just in case. My mom also came out for a few days to help Ray get things ready and set up the nursery.

It was brutal lying there day after day without knowing what was ahead. But I kept coming back to one passage in my Bible again and again:

> Don't worry about anything; instead, pray about
> everything. Tell God what you need, and thank him
> for all he has done. Then you will experience God's
> peace, which exceeds anything we can understand.
> His peace will guard your hearts and minds as you
> live in Christ Jesus.[1]

I have to admit that it was hard not to worry about what might happen. But I also knew that stressing myself out wasn't going to help my situation or the baby's. And what was the point of worrying? I had been through enough by now to know that if it was God's will for our baby to be born with Down syndrome, there was a reason, and it was good. After all, weren't all babies perfect? And surely God wouldn't entrust a child with special needs to Ray and me if we weren't capable of taking care of those needs and giving that child a rich and wonderful life, would He?

Despite all my fears—or perhaps because of them—my relationship with God had never been stronger than it was during those final few weeks. I told Him about every doubt, fear, and concern as it arose. And I'm not proud to admit that there were a lot of them. But just knowing God was present and aware of everything I was going through gave me such an incredible sense of peace. I wasn't alone. He was there. He was going to take care of me, and He was going to take care of our little baby. He was going to take care of *everything*. He always did.

As my due date drew closer, I grew more excited about meeting this amazing little person inside me. There was only one small problem: Our baby didn't want to come out. I'd spent 12 weeks on bed rest, and now that it was showtime, we couldn't get the baby to budge.

We tried everything—long, warm showers . . . spicy foods—Ray and I even spent several afternoons walking up and down the hills by our house. Nothing. So when Dr. Margolin said it was time to induce labor, Ray poured me into the front of the car, stretched my seat belt to its limit, and drove us to the hospital.

After 36 hours of intense labor, I was still pregnant. And exhausted. And in tears.

Dr. Margolin was a saint. "Jodi, honey," he said, rubbing my back (by the way . . . that didn't work either), "you've done everything you can do, and I'm so proud of you, but we need to get this baby out."

Ray and I'd had our hearts set on a natural delivery, but now that I was in what felt like my 14th month, *how* had taken a back seat to *now*.

"Okay," I said, nodding. "Just do whatever you have to do."

That's when everything went south. The baby's heart rate started to drop, and the next thing I knew, they were paging the emergency C-section team. I was moved to a gurney and rushed down the hall toward the delivery room. Poor Ray, also exhausted, was stumbling alongside us, trying to pull his scrubs on without tripping over himself. My dearest friend, Marcia, was two steps behind him, video camera in hand, taping the whole thing, and in the midst of all the chaos, the *only* thing running through my head was, *Awww, shoot! It's January 6—my niece's birthday. I was trying to avoid that.* Way to stay calm in a crisis.

Ten minutes later, Dr. Margolin *finally* delivered the news we'd been waiting months to hear: "It's a boy!"

"Is he okay?" I asked.

"He's amazing."

Our newborn was also silent. I looked over at Ray. His eyes were locked like lasers on the NICU team huddled at the foot of my bed. Then I saw Marcia lower the camera and turn it off. The silence lasted almost two full minutes, during which I don't think Ray or I took a single breath. Then suddenly, there was a tiny yelp, followed by a long, loud, beautiful scream. McKinley Raymond Benson had finally arrived.

I looked back up at Ray, tears streaming down my face. "Is he really okay?"

"He's beautiful, sweetie," Ray choked out in between tears.

After what felt like ages, they brought him over to me and laid him on my chest. Ray was right. Our baby *was* beautiful—absolutely beautiful. I don't know if the markers had been wrong or if God had intervened. Either way, I was grateful.

~~~~~~~~~

Once Ray and I welcomed this new little life into our house, I wanted us to get a fresh start. I had been thinking about it for a while, but it wasn't until McKinley was born that I decided to talk to Ray about it. So one night, after we had gotten McKinley down, I just put it out there.

"Ray, what would you think about renewing our vows? We could combine it with McKinley's christening. All our close friends and family will be coming out to LA for that anyway."

He didn't even bat an eyelash. "I love that idea." I had a feeling he might. Ray had always been a huge sentimentalist, and after everything we'd been through over the past year, I think we both felt like a little celebration was in order.

It ended up being a lovely evening. I had picked out a beautiful cream-colored gown, and Ray had bought a cream suit to match. One of his best friends, Keith Boyd, our former pastor in New York, came out to perform the renewal ceremony. It was especially fitting because he knew us both well and had been there for most of our journey. And our current pastor from LA, who had been with us through the entire pregnancy, did the christening. The weather was perfect, so everybody gathered on our patio overlooking the hills. There were flowers on every table, and we even had a wedding cake.

But as beautiful as it was, that evening wasn't about the dress, or the flowers, or the cake. It was about promises—to each other and to God. When Ray and I had come to the edge of a cliff, God promised me that He wasn't finished with us yet. And He wasn't—not by a long shot.

I had come *so* close to throwing everything away—my marriage, my life—but through it all, God had remained faithful. He was there during my darkest hour—forgiving, reassuring, and loving me back from the brink. And I am so unthinkably grateful for that. Just look at everything I would have missed out on—a wonderful husband; a happy marriage; a beautiful, healthy little boy; and about a thousand other blessings, none of which I deserved. That's what that evening was about. Ray and I had both grown so much and come so far over the past 15 years. We wanted to honor that and to make those vows again, but in a different light. Because now, more than ever, I understood what they really meant.

20

*"Authority Should Derive
from the Consent of the Governed,
Not from the Threat of Force!"*

Generally speaking, I'm not a big red-carpet gal. I absolutely love meeting people—especially kids—and getting to hear all about their favorite *Mermaid* memories and moments. In fact, I don't want to brag, but I may have the most stared-at legs at Disney World.

Ray, the kids, and I are big Disney Park people (both Disney World and Disneyland), so we're there all the time. We just love the roller coasters, especially Expedition Everest. Gosh, we'll do Everest 12 times in a row. We're kind of crazy that way. We've done this ride in the pouring rain, in intense heat, in the freezing cold—we don't care. We just love it. Anyway, whenever we go to one of the parks as part of a work function, Disney blesses us with a wonderful VIP tour guide. As soon as people see visitors walking with the person in the plaid vest, they always take a closer look.

Usually the parents figure it out first. Then they'll crouch down next to their little guy or girl, point up at me, and say, "That's the voice of Ariel." Because I don't look like Ariel, the kids are usually a little skeptical, and at some point, almost all of them will look down at my legs. It's so adorable. I can almost see the little wheels turning as they try to figure out, *Where's her tail?* But as soon as they hear my voice . . . it's like magic.

I get it. It's quite a leap for a three-, four-, or five-year-old. Even my own kids took a few minutes to piece it together. I waited until they were each about two and a half so it wouldn't freak them out too much. Then I just popped the tape in the VCR, stood next to the TV, and when Ariel came on, said, "Watch . . . Mommy makes the voice." Then I started singing and saying the lines right alongside Ariel. It was so sweet. Their eyes darted back and forth between me and the screen. Then *ding!* The light went on, their little faces lit up, and they were like, "Mommy is Ariel!" followed almost immediately by "Why isn't your hair red anymore?"

I love working with kids—especially the really little ones, because they ask the cutest questions, like "Where's Flounder?" and "Does your dad know you're here?" and "Does your tail grow back when you go under water?"

One time I was a special guest in my niece's third grade class, and I was telling her classmates all about animation— how they do the sketches, how we record the voices, and the whole process of putting *The Little Mermaid* together. When I finished, I asked if anyone had any questions, and one little boy raised his hand and said, "How do you hold your breath underwater for so long?" (By the way, in case you're wondering, as a mermaid, I can breathe under water. I have that ability.) It's kind of like Santa Claus. At some point, they figure it out, but until they do, gosh, is it fun!

But back to the red carpet . . . when it comes to work, I'm not really into all the glitz and glamour. I just like to get in, get my job done, and get back home to my family. That's part of what makes voice-over work ideal for me. Because so much of it is done in isolation, you can practically control your own schedule. That said, I never turn down an opportunity to go to a premiere or special screening, because more often than not, it's the first, and sometimes *only*, chance I get to actually meet my costars face-to-face.

I don't know if you've ever noticed, but the end of the closing credits of all Pixar movies includes a list of "Production Babies," which is basically a roll call of all the children born to the cast and crew while the movie was being made. As it happened, for *Toy Story 2*, McKinley was one of those babies, so naturally I brought him with me to the premiere. He was about 10 months old at the time, and I had him hiked up on my hip. As I made my way down the carpet, I noticed Tom Hanks standing off to the side talking with a few members of the press corps. Since we never got a chance to meet during the actual production, I figured I'd introduce myself. Besides, kids *love* Tom, and I thought McKinley would get a kick out of hearing him do Woody.

So I walked over and said, "Hi, my name's Jodi. I did the voice for Barbie," and he could not have been sweeter. He leaned in, looked McKinley right in the eye, and said, "Hey, little fella. What's your name?" Well, as if on cue, McKinley's little face turned beet red, and he burst into tears. Of course, being the wonderful mother that I am, I said, "Oh, we gotta get a picture of this." But McKinley was so freaked out that poor Tom had to duck behind us and stick his head into the shot like he was photobombing us. It was priceless.

Now Tom hadn't done anything wrong. I cannot stress that enough. My theory (and I'm sticking with this) is that Tom was sporting a full beard at the time, and none of our friends *had* beards, so McKinley had never seen one before. Tom was also wearing dark sunglasses, and I think our little guy just didn't know what to make of it—hence the hysterics.

I still have that picture, and I love it, if for no other reason than it's an awesome reminder not to rush to judgment or put too much stock in first impressions. How else can you explain my angelic son screaming bloody murder at one of the most lovable figures in film?

Coincidentally, that's also why I loved being the voice of Barbie.

Poor Barbie has taken a lot of heat over the years for being too thin, too ditzy, and too materialistic. So when Disney/ Pixar approached Mattel about using Barbie in the *Toy Story* franchise, the Mattel folks were adamant that she not be portrayed as a caricature. They wanted her to come across as bright, well-versed, and genuine. They even sent a representative out to my first recording session to make sure we got it right.

"This is a really big deal," the rep said. "This is the first time Barbie has ever had a voice, and we want to make sure we go about it in a very respectful way."

I could not have agreed with her more—with one tiny exception.

"Actually," I explained, "Barbie *has* had a voice before. In fact, I did it." It's true. Shortly after *Mermaid* released,

I was asked to do Barbie's speaking voice for *Dance! Workout with Barbie*, a 30-minute exercise video for kids.

"You're kidding."

Why would I joke about this?

"Nope. That was me."

That seemed to reassure them a little. I mean, really, what are the odds? I don't even think John Lasseter or Lee Unkrich, who directed *Toy Story 2*, knew I'd done the Barbie video. At one point, I flat out asked them, "So . . . why me?" They just said they really liked what I had done with Ariel and thought Barbie was "in there somewhere." Now we just had to figure out how to get her out.

So my first day in the studio, John and Lee brought out a big box of Barbie dolls, and we just started playing with them. I had a few pages of the script, so I started experimenting with some different voices while they recorded it. Honestly, the biggest challenge was trying to get her to sound warm and friendly, because bodywise, she's kind of stiff. She can't really use her hands when she speaks, which I do constantly, and because her arms bend only at the elbows, she moves pretty robotically. She also has much better posture than I've ever had. That said, I could understand why the Mattel people were concerned. They wanted her to sound vulnerable and real, and it's hard to move like that and not sound fake or mechanical.

In the end, we landed on a bubbly yet confident voice. What really broke Barbie out of the mold, though, was the way Disney/Pixar presented her.

In *Toy Story 2*, she's introduced as Tour Guide Barbie. That's important, because while all the other dolls are dancing and doing the limbo by the pool, Tour Guide Barbie has an actual job. Not only that, she's also really good at it! She's extremely knowledgeable about all the other toys in Al's Toy Barn and is even aware of a marketing gaffe back in 1995, when "shortsighted retailers did not order enough dolls to meet demand,"[1] hence the entire aisle dedicated to extra Buzz Lightyears. I mean, where would a Barbie doll gain a working knowledge of merchandising and consumer demand?

That's one of the things I have always loved about the Toy Story movies: They're created with both kids and adults in mind. Not only do a lot of the toys, like Slinky Dog and Mr. and Mrs. Potato Head, date back to the fifties and sixties—when most of the parents in the audience would have been kids themselves—but a lot of the jokes and dialogue are geared toward an adult audience as well.

I think my favorite Barbie line from *Toy Story 2*, though, is the one where she tells Hamm, Rex, Slinky, and Mr. Potato Head to "please keep your hands, arms, and accessories inside the car," and about a minute later to "remain seated, please," which she then repeats in Spanish. Kids won't get why that's funny, but any parent who has ever been to Disneyland as a kid will immediately recognize it as something that was said at the beginning of every ride. I love it when they do stuff like that.

People tend to think of Woody and Buzz as the heroes of the Toy Story franchise, but really it's Barbie who comes to the rescue in *Toy Story 3*. Sure, she starts off, much as you might suspect, crying over being abandoned by the little girl she belonged to and then falling in love with Ken at first sight. But as soon as she discovers that her friends are in trouble and Ken is involved, she drops him like a hot potato and starts hatching a plan to save the toys. By the way, her plan? It's pretty ingenious. She not only tricks Ken into telling her about how Lotso, the strawberry bear, reset Buzz to his original factory settings but also overpowers Ken, ties him up, and blackmails him into telling her where Buzz's instruction manual is, which she gets back. If anything, Ken is the one who ends up looking kind of silly. How's that for flipping the script?

But that's not even the best part.

I've had a lot of great lines over the years, but I don't think any of them come close to the one Barbie fires off at Lotso when he corners her and her toy friends. And Disney/Pixar sets it up beautifully. Right after a very emotional Jessie calls Lotso "a liar and a bully" for the way he treats the toys, Barbie steps forward, and with all the clarity and conviction in the world, declares, "Jessie's right! Authority should derive from the consent of the governed, not from the threat of force."

Seriously, who saw that coming? My guess is the audience is about as thunderstruck as Hamm and Mr. Potato Head, who practically do a double take in response. I think it's safe to say, nobody looks at Barbie quite the same way after that.

The point is, it's so easy to make assumptions about people based on their looks, their faith, their political beliefs, or a single brief encounter, and wow, can that be dangerous.

I remember when I first met Michael Keaton, who did the voice of Ken. I was walking into the studio for a recording session as he was leaving. Naturally, I was excited to see him. After all, we were Ken and Barbie. Imagine my surprise, then, when he wouldn't come within 10 feet of me. It turns out the poor guy was as sick as a dog and contagious, and he didn't want me to catch anything. So we just waved at each other from a distance and said a super quick hello, and that was it.

Of course, when we ran into each other again a few months later at a publicity event, we made up for the missed opportunity. In fact, we spent the better part of the day together, taking pictures, doing interviews—I think we even re-created a scene or two from the movie. That's not to say he was rude the first time we met; far from it. It just wasn't the magical "Dream Weaver" moment it was in the movie.

~~~~~~~

A few years ago, Ray and I were at Disneyland with the kids, and as usual, I was wearing my circa 1999 "Disney Mom" fanny pack. I've always got that with me because I don't like to put anything in the front pocket of a ride. Ever. Well, I must have been taking a few last-second pictures of the kids, because instead of putting my phone back in my fanny pack, I slipped it into that little Velcro pocket in front of me on the ride. It was a classic rookie mistake. And I can promise you, this was *not* our first trip to Disneyland. (It wasn't even our first trip that year.)

Anyway, after the ride ended, we decided to grab some ice cream. As I was standing in line at the ice cream parlor, I reached into my fanny pack and realized my phone was missing. Now, my phone has roughly 132,000 photos on it—I kid you not. I am a photo fanatic. I have documented every waking moment of our kids' lives for more than a decade. I just love scrolling back through old photos and reminiscing about all the special moments we've had together as a family. And it's not just me; the kids love looking at them too. It's probably genetic.

Well, my heart just sank, and before I knew it, I started tearing up.

"Honey, it's okay," Ray assured me. "Everything's on the iCloud. You haven't lost anything."

All of a sudden, I felt someone tap my shoulder. I turned around and saw the sweetest young lady standing behind me.

"I'm sorry," she said, "but are you Jodi Benson?"

"Yes, I am."

"Could I possibly bother you for a picture?"

I felt so terrible. Normally I would say, "Absolutely!" Photo fanatic, remember? But at that particular moment, I just could not get it together.

"I'm so sorry," I sniffed. "But I just lost my phone, and it has my whole life on it. I'm so, so sorry. I just can't."

She was very understanding. She assured me it was okay, apologized for bothering me, and said that she hoped I'd find my phone. Poor thing. She had no idea I was upset until I turned around, and by then it was too late.

Now my kids were completely shocked. That was the first time they had ever seen me say no to anyone for anything at a Disney park. I wish I had a picture of their faces.

See? Now you know why I was so devastated.

Well, by this point, our amazing VIP guide was retracing our steps through the park, trying to figure out where I might have left my phone, and I was tucked away in a corner behind a trash can, quietly sobbing and praying, *God, I know this is just a silly little thing, but it means so much to me.* The kids sat at a nearby table eating their ice cream, trying to figure out who this hysterical woman was and what she'd done with their mother.

Fast-forward five minutes that felt like five years. In ran my tour guide with my phone in his hand. I collapsed in relief— thanking my wonderful guide, thanking God, hugging the kids. I promise you, never has that little ice cream parlor known so much drama.

Tragedy averted, I dried my face, took a few deep breaths, and headed outside to rejoin the world. And there she was—the poor girl who had so sweetly asked for a photo—sitting at an outside table eating her ice cream.

I went straight over to her and said, "I am so sorry for the way I behaved in there just now. I've never said no to a picture before. I just . . ."

"Oh no, no, no," she broke in. "I totally get it. It's okay, really."

"Thank you. I appreciate that." Seriously, I could have hugged her. "Would you still like a picture?"

Thankfully she did. I can't tell you how grateful I was that I found her, because honestly, I would have worn that on my heart for ages. Mostly, though, I'm grateful she didn't let one unfortunate moment with me forever color the way she thought of Ariel. Disney fans really are the best.

It takes time to get to know people—I mean, *really* know them. Learning who someone is as a person requires a lot of active engagement and conversation. It takes real discernment to decipher the things that matter most—like kindness, character, honesty, and integrity—and it doesn't happen instantly. In the meantime, we need to be a little slower to judge and a little more open to showing grace.

Sometimes it feels like all it takes is for someone to disagree with us about one thing, and that's it—game over. That kind of attitude has always bothered me, because it implies we can be in relationship only with people who are exactly like us. But what would be the fun of that? I have several friends who don't think the same way or believe in the same things I do. That's what makes our friendships so rich—we can learn from each other.

As a general rule of thumb, I try to think the very best of someone until I have reason to believe otherwise. I just try to pay attention, listen to their heart, and watch for signs pointing to their true character. Like, when I walk away after spending time with them, do I feel built up, encouraged, and closer to God, or do I feel beaten up, used, and less than? Is this friendship going to bear good, healthy fruit and make me a better person, or is it going to suck the life out of me so that I'm no good to anyone? Once you've gotten to know a person's heart, the decision of whether to welcome them into your life or walk away becomes a lot easier.

By the way, in case you've forgotten, Ken and Barbie end up together. Ken had never really been a bad guy; he'd just been a hapless pawn in Lotso's quest for power. Luckily for him, Barbie was intelligent and discerning enough to realize the truth. And for all his shortcomings, Ken was smart enough to realize that Barbie wasn't just another pretty face. She was something special.

Who are we kidding? They're a great couple. I'd go to their wedding in a heartbeat—even if there was a red carpet. Goodness knows, I've got the legs for it.

21

~~~~~~

"I Don't Know When, I Don't Know How"

By this point you're probably thinking, *Gosh, this gal's led a pretty charmed life.* Yeah . . . no. Just because I work for the most magical place on earth doesn't mean my life has been a fairy tale. I have been on the receiving end of some truly wonderful blessings, but I've also had my share of heartaches.

About eight months after McKinley was born, Ray and I got pregnant again. And once again, we were over the moon. We always knew we wanted to have two kids. Selfishly, I wanted one of each—if for no other reason than I had all this fun *Mermaid* stuff at home, and I wanted a little princess of my own to share it with. But given my age and history, all we really cared about was having a healthy baby.

Everything started off wonderfully. My usual morning (and afternoon and evening) sickness aside, I felt great. Then when I was about ten and a half weeks along, I went in to see Dr. Margolin for my regular checkup. I was chattering away as he went, telling him all about McKinley's latest exploits, when I noticed his expression suddenly shift from cheerful and relaxed to solemn and concerned.

"Is there something wrong?" I held my breath.

He looked at me tenderly. "Jodi . . ."

Oh no.

"I'm so sorry, but I'm not getting a heartbeat."

I was devastated. There had been no symptoms. No signs. Nothing.

"I don't understand. What happened? What went wrong?"

But there were no answers. Sometimes bad things just happen.

A few days later, Ray and I came back to Dr. Margolin's office. Our first miscarriage happened early enough that it resolved on its own. This one, however, required some help. Unfortunately, because I was still nursing McKinley, they weren't able to put me under, so I was awake for the entire procedure. Ray was right there with me, but still I sobbed uncontrollably the entire time. It was nightmarish—so much so that if I had it to do over again, I would demand to be put under, and I would spare Ray from having to be in the room. No parent should have to go through that.

As much as we tried to make sense of it, we just couldn't. Part of me even wondered if I was being punished for something. *But what?* That didn't feel like the God I knew. The God I knew was a God of comfort and forgiveness. He understood what it felt like to lose a child. And because He understood, I knew He could handle every raw, unfiltered emotion I could throw at Him.

And I did.

I cried. I yelled. I questioned. I screamed. And in the midst of all that crying out, I could feel His presence. I could hear His voice in my heart telling me to trust Him.

And I did.

The only other option was to walk away from my faith, and *that* was not an option. Not for me, anyway.

I believe wholeheartedly in the promise of Romans 8:28: "We know that God causes everything to work together for the good of those who love God and are called according to his purpose for them." God can make *anything* good.

Look at *Smile*. The whole production was a nightmare: Frank Rich hated it, and even today it's regarded as one of Broadway's biggest flops. But if it hadn't been for that show, I never would have met Howard, I wouldn't have auditioned for Disney, I wouldn't have been cast as Ariel, and I wouldn't have met Cindy, Glen and Linda, or Buster and Gina, all of whom have become cherished lifelong friends. The show itself might have been a failure, but look at all the good that came out of it!

Loss is hard. Sometimes it doesn't make any sense. You just have to trust that if there is good to be found, God will find it.

In the days following the procedure, Dr. Margolin and his team ran a whole battery of tests to try to figure out what had gone wrong and why all my pregnancies had been so difficult. And they *did* find something.

It turns out I have a condition called antiphospholipid syndrome (APS), which basically means that my blood identifies the baby's blood as a foreign object and tries to get rid of it. I also have a poorly positioned fibroid cyst that grows to roughly the size of a fist during pregnancy. When I was carrying McKinley, it became lodged between his head and neck, which is why I wasn't able to deliver him naturally.

The bad news was, I was still high risk. The good news, however, was now that we knew what was wrong, we could do something about it.

Three months after our second miscarriage, we were ready to try again, and with the help of some fertility medication, we were blessed with another pregnancy. As soon as I found out I was expecting, I started giving myself daily heparin shots to counteract the APS. The shots had to be given in the abdomen, which was incredibly painful, and by my ninth month I was completely bruised along both sides—but it worked. I also started seeing Dr. Margolin every two weeks so he could monitor the growth and position of the cyst via ultrasound. We even had a specific plan for the birth itself. Since we knew the fibroid cyst was going to be a problem, Dr. Margolin ruled out the option of a natural birth and scheduled a C-section.

"We almost lost both of you with McKinley," he cautioned. "There's no point in putting either of you at risk again—especially now that we know what we're dealing with."

We were so much more prepared this time around and had the date on the calendar weeks in advance. Ray and I got a good night's sleep and drove in first thing that morning. Ray's sister, Deb, came out to watch two-and-a-half-year-old McKinley until we got back. Best of all, there was no extended labor, no unforeseen complications, and no emergency NICU teams racing down the hospital corridor at 3 a.m. Everything was calm, orderly, and completely drama-free. It was the *Crazy for You* of deliveries.

The only unknown going into the delivery was whether McKinley was going to have a little brother or a little sister. Again, I would have been thrilled either way, but deep in my heart, I *so* wanted a little girl. In fact, a few days before I went into the hospital, I had this incredibly vivid dream about a little girl with long blonde braids who was wearing bib overalls. Now whether that dream was just a wish my heart made or it came straight from God, I don't know. All I do know is that when Dr. Margolin announced that we'd had a little girl, Ray and I both fell to pieces.

She was so precious. She didn't even come out screaming. Instead, she came out cooing like a dove, as though she had just woken up, looked at us, and said, "Oh, there you are!"

We had originally planned on naming her Lily, but by the time she was born, it felt like there were Lilys everywhere. As it happened, Ray had recently been in touch with an old college friend whose niece had just beaten cancer, and her name was Delaney. We loved that name. And we loved that the little girl it came from was a fighter.

Four days later, we took Delaney Leighton Benson home wearing a little pink onesie. Believe it or not, Disney hadn't licensed any *Little Mermaid* outfits for newborns back then. Talk about a missed marketing opportunity.

If not for our miscarriage—as hellish as it had been—we never would have known about the APS or the fibroid cyst, I wouldn't have been monitored as closely, we wouldn't have known to schedule a C-section, and we might not have our beautiful girl.

God works all things for our benefit. I really do believe that—even if I can't always see it.

Likewise, a few years ago, I had the opportunity to use

some of my Disney connections for good. It was a surprise for my niece Kylie. We were extremely close. In fact, Kylie and her family—her parents, Mark and Robin Myers, and her three sisters—were a big reason Ray and I eventually decided to settle in Georgia. Kylie was just a year younger than Delaney, and McKinley was sandwiched right in between Kylie's two oldest sisters. They all got along beautifully, and Ray and I loved the idea of our kids growing up surrounded by cousins—hence the move.

Shortly after her 12th birthday, Kylie was diagnosed with Ewing sarcoma, a rare and highly aggressive form of bone cancer. Most kids would fall apart after receiving that kind of diagnosis, and understandably so. But not Kylie. She had the most positive attitude of anyone I've ever met. And I think a lot of that came from her faith. When she got her diagnosis, instead of crying, screaming, or yelling, she very calmly and quietly turned to her parents and said, "God must have great big plans for me."

Also, she had just walked her best friend, Bailey, through a similar diagnosis and treatment. I mean, what are the odds that in a class of 16 kids, there would be two girls with rare pediatric bone cancers? By the time Kylie was diagnosed, Bailey was in complete remission with absolutely no evidence of the disease in her body.

So in Kylie's mind, this was just a bump in the road and a chance for her to help encourage other kids who were going through the same thing, just as she had done for Bailey. In fact, her number one goal throughout her entire battle was "to make God smile."

Kylie made everyone smile. Even when the brutal side effects of her chemotherapy were taking their toll, she somehow managed to find joy and laughter. She explained her positive attitude this way: "I think cancer should die, not the kids." I have never seen anyone—at any age—handle a catastrophic illness as beautifully, as heroically, and as joyfully as Kylie did.

Now, I love every one of my cousins, nieces, and nephews dearly, but Kylie had always held a special place in my heart, in part because we shared the same passion for musical theatre. Much like mine at her age, Kylie's dream was to perform on Broadway, and believe me, this kid had the goods. I could see it when she was only two years old. The personality, the talent, the voice, the presence—she was the whole package.

Kylie used to tell me that she dreamed about performing on Broadway one day, so when she was getting close to finishing her treatment, I reached out to my friends at Disney and the Make-A-Wish Foundation in Atlanta, and together we arranged for Kylie to appear onstage in Disney's Broadway musical *Aladdin*.

They went all out, designing a costume and creating a special wig just for her. They were even going to let her take part in a full-dress rehearsal—the whole nine yards. The performance was scheduled to take place right after Kylie finished her final round of radiation and rang the bell signaling the end of 11 months of hell and the beginning of her journey of healing.

Kylie knew about the performance, but what she didn't know was that as an extra special surprise, Ray, our kids, and I had already bought our plane tickets and were all going to be there when that curtain came up and Kylie got to experience her five minutes of glory. To be honest, I think we were almost as excited as she was. And what wasn't there to be excited about? It had been a horrific year, and as brutal as Kylie's treatment had been, it had done its job. As of her last scan, Kylie was completely cancer-free.

That's when the unthinkable happened.

A few days before we were scheduled to fly out to New York, I was driving home from the grocery store, and my phone rang. It was Mark.

"Hey, Mark," I chirped. "Everything's all set. How's Kylie? Is she excited?"

"Where are you right now?"

My heart beat a little faster. "I'm in the car. Why?"

"You need to pull over."

Something was definitely wrong. I could hear it in his voice. I quickly drove the car to the side of the road, put it in park, and flipped on the hazards. "Okay . . . I'm stopped. What's happening?"

"It's done. The cancer is everywhere. It's all over her body from head to toe."

"What?" I couldn't wrap my head around it. *This isn't possible. The last set of scans showed it was gone. The treatment worked. God healed her.*

Mark's voice sounded absolutely hollow. "She wants to stay home. The trip is canceled."

I just sat there frozen, staring blankly through the windshield, tears streaming down my cheeks. "Is there anything I can do?"

What more *could* I do? Over the past 11 months, I had done everything I could think of. I had anointed this child with oil. I had prayed and fasted for her. I had pleaded with God. I had cried out to God. I had wailed to God. I'd been on my knees before God. I'd been on my face before God. God had even given me visions of her being completely restored and healed. How could this have happened? How could she have gone from cancer-free to completely covered in less than 48 hours?

"You need to come. You, Ray, and the kids. Today if possible. We want to make sure everybody has some good quality time with her while she's still awake."

Later that day, we loaded up the car, and the four of us drove down to Mark and Robin's place in Suwanee—unfathomably, to say goodbye.

I wanted so badly to put on a brave face and not upset Kylie, but as soon as I walked in the room, my heart just shattered. I could barely even speak. I sat on the edge of the bed, told her I loved her repeatedly, and wept. The next thing I knew, Kylie was gently patting my head.

"It's okay, Aunt Jodi. Everything's gonna be okay."

No, it wouldn't. Not in my mind, anyway. Nothing about this was okay. I was a mess. But Kylie was perfectly calm. It was almost as though Jesus Himself were holding her tight and giving her that peace that surpasses all human understanding. She wasn't angry or sad or upset; she was perfectly content.

I wasn't. I couldn't bear the thought of losing her. Ray, the kids, and I spent a few days with Kylie. I wanted to stay longer, but I had a concert scheduled in Milwaukee that weekend. We had originally planned to fly out as a family right after Kylie's performance, then stay over for a few extra days to visit with my mom and sister. I offered to stay and sit with Kylie—however long she wanted, but she wouldn't hear of it.

"I want you to go to your concert, Aunt Jodi," she insisted. "I want you to sing 'Part of Your World' for me. And I want you to tell Neena [my mom] that I love her very much."

"I will, sweetie," I promised her. "I will."

Ray stayed behind to support Robin and Mark while the kids and I went on to Milwaukee. We knew that by the time we got home, Kylie would probably be gone. It was heart-wrenching not being there. But I'd made her a promise, and I was going to keep it. It's what she wanted—for us to go on with our lives, to be with the ones we loved, and to do what made us happiest.

Kylie passed away that same night as I was singing "Part of Your World" during my dress rehearsal. Ray had texted me the news, and I saw it as soon as I finished singing. It was a week and a half before her 13th birthday, and one day after she was supposed to appear on Broadway.

How do you wrap your mind around that? I don't know that you can. I couldn't. I still can't.

Losing Kylie was the first time in my Christian life that something hadn't worked out the way I thought it should. Her death just felt cruel. It would have been easier if God had said very clearly from day one, "I'm going to take her home. This is My plan." But to go from one extreme to the other in the blink of an eye—to give everyone hope and then snatch it away—I just didn't have a place for that.

It's one thing when someone passes away in their eighties or nineties after having lived a long and fruitful life. I can make sense of that. But Kylie was only 12. She still had her whole life ahead of her. What was the point of her death?

For that matter, what was the point of prayer? I'd prayed night and day for God to heal Kylie, but it hadn't worked.

It was the first time I felt as though my prayers went unanswered, and that was a massive blow to my faith. One of my closest friends, Angela Ewers, is a grief counselor, and she had an interesting perspective. "What if Kylie had different prayers than you did," she suggested, "and God chose to answer hers instead?"

I had never considered that. Maybe what we wanted wasn't what Kylie wanted. I do believe Jesus was holding her tightly those last few days. Maybe she got a taste of what heaven was like and decided, "I'm ready! Let's go!" Maybe that's what she asked God for on that final day. I don't know. I'll probably never know. And that is *so* hard.

I can look back at other difficult times in my life and say, "Oh yeah, that was a terrible season, but look what God did with it!" Yet when we lost Kylie, I just couldn't see the good. I still can't. Childhood cancer has not been cured. Money has been raised in her honor for research, but I've yet to see the fruit of that research, nor have I seen any significant changes in chemo for children. So where is it? Where's the good? When am I going to see it?

That's hard for a believer—to look for the good in a bad situation and say, "I can't see it." When it comes to Kylie, I don't know if I ever will. And do you know what? I'm not sure that God finds it necessary for me to understand.

Earlier I mentioned that life's difficulties are easier to accept when I consider Romans 8:28, which states that God promises all circumstances will "work together for the good of those who love God and are called according to his purpose." Sometimes I can see the positive that results from a disappointment (as with all the friendships that came out of *Smile*), but Kylie's death made me realize that I won't always see how the good plays out during my time on earth. It's entirely possible I may not see the fruit of Kylie's passing until I'm in heaven myself. I can accept that, but I still don't like it.

I wish God had written this story differently, but there's nothing I can do. Actually, there is *one* thing I can do. I can do what Kylie did. In spite of all the fear, the uncertainty, and the pain, I can choose joy.

Every day when I wake up, I have a choice to make: I can choose to have a lousy, rotten, stinking day. I can choose to be unkind. I can choose to wallow. I can choose to pout. I can choose to be immobilized by grief. Or I can choose joy. I can choose laughter. I can choose love.

I can spend my days shaking my fist and asking God, "Why did this happen?" or I can follow Kylie's lead—keeping my hands and heart open and asking God, "How can I make You smile today?"

I can't change the past, and only God holds the future. All I have is today. So if it would please God, let me love well today. Let me serve well today. And when I put my head on the pillow tonight, let me be able to tell myself, *You know what? Today was a good day. I got to love on a friend. I got to love on my kids. I got to stop and pray for somebody. I got to send someone a text that said, "Really thinking about you today. Love you, miss you, hope you're doing okay."*

And for now, that's enough. It has to be.

I know they say that time heals all wounds, but it doesn't. Losing Kylie still hurts, and it gets worse every year that she's gone and every day that I can't see the good. And yet I choose to believe. Because as sad as my life is without Kylie, life without my faith would be even worse. Faith is what gives me hope. It's what makes the pain bearable. And it's how I know with certainty that good *will* come from Kylie's passing—even though I may not get to see it on this side of heaven. After all, at its core, that's what faith is—believing in something you can't see.

At least not yet.

22

"*Just beyond the Meadows of Joy and the Valley of Contentment*"

"I have no idea what I'm doing."

It's astonishing how much of my life can be summed up by that simple sentence.

"Don't worry about it, Jodi. You're gonna be fine." That was a pretty bold prediction, considering I hadn't even gotten out of the makeup chair yet. I had just flown to New York to help an old friend of mine, Kevin Lima, with a new live-action/animated movie called *Enchanted*. Kevin had been one of the animators on *The Little Mermaid*, and because the film was kind of an homage to the classic Disney princess story, Kevin had this fantastic idea of having a few of the actual Disney princesses do surprise cameos throughout.

It was really very clever. Paige played an actress in a TV soap opera that was on in the background of one particular scene, and Judy Kuhn, who provided the singing voice of Pocahontas, played an overwhelmed mom who lives in the main character's building. As for me, I was Sam, the secretary of the male lead. I was super excited because it was the first time I had ever done a live-action feature film. The only problem was that I had absolutely no idea what I was doing.

In fact, I almost turned it down. I was homeschooling both kids at that point, and Delaney's birthday bumped right up against the filming schedule. But it was a Disney project, and Kevin was a friend, and he gave me his word that I would be finished and back on a plane in time for Delaney's birthday. Plus I was under the impression that Patrick Duffy was going to be involved. I watched *Dallas* all the time when I was growing up, and I figured it would be a real kick to get to work with Bobby Ewing.

Anyway, after they did my hair and makeup, I wandered out to the lobby of the beautiful, 40-story, all-glass office building where we were going to be filming. There was a massive saltwater aquarium set up in the reception area where I was told to wait, and just as I was about to head over to look at the fish, I noticed Kevin walking toward me with a very nice-looking, dark-haired guy in a business suit.

"Jodi," Kevin said, "this is Patrick. Patrick, Jodi."

Well, the guy reaches his hand out and says, "Hi, Jodi, nice to meet you," and all I can think is, *That's not Patrick Duffy.*

"Hi, Patrick. It's nice to meet you too." Then I leaned over and whispered, "I'm sorry. I really don't know what I'm doing. I'm just here with Disney."

He was very sweet. It turned out he had a daughter

about the same age as Delaney, and she was a *huge* Ariel fan. I wanted to ask his last name, but I was already self-conscious enough. Besides, they had shut down the whole lobby so we could film this scene, and I got the impression they were anxious to keep things moving. Fortunately, I was a total pro at this.

It was like *Mermaid* all over again. I kept flailing my hands, only instead of smacking the mic, this time I kept blocking the camera. Of course, in my defense, I had no idea where the camera was. Eventually Kevin came over and said, "Okay, Jodi, when you see the red light—"

"I'm sorry," I stopped him. "What red light are you talking about?"

"That one over there," he said, pointing to a bright red light on top of one of the cameras. "When the light goes on, it means the camera is filming, so try not to stand or wave your hand in front of it, okay?"

"Oh, I'm sorry. I didn't realize—"

"No, no, no, no—you're fine. Just watch out for the camera." He could not have been more gracious. And God bless Patrick Dempsey. It was obvious he knew what he was doing, and he was so patient while I tried to figure it out. Fortunately I only made two or three tiny mistakes. Then they had a problem with one of the lights (which I swear I didn't touch), so we took a break. That's when I noticed dozens of women standing with their faces pressed up against the glass on every single floor, watching us like hawks.

I nodded up at them and asked Patrick, "What's that all about?"

He looked up, then kind of awkwardly said, "They're just *Grey's* fans."

"*Grey's?*" I asked. Seriously—could I have been more clueless?

"*Grey's Anatomy,*" he said almost apologetically. "It's a show I've been on for a while."

"Oh, that's cool. I'm sorry, I really don't watch much TV," I explained. "I have two kids, and I homeschool them both, so most of my time is spent preparing lesson plans and—"

"Really?" he interrupted. "That's interesting. Do you live in LA?"

"We used to, but a couple of years ago we moved to a beautiful little spot near the mountains of North Georgia. My husband has a lot of family there, and we really wanted the kids to grow up around their cousins. Plus it's just a gorgeous area. We're right on a lake. The kids just love it."

The weird thing was, Patrick seemed genuinely interested. It turned out he and his wife had also been thinking for a while about getting away from LA. He told me he collected race cars and wanted to find a place out in the country where he could have more room for them. It's amazing what you learn when you actually get a chance to work with somebody in person.

Every time we took a little break, Patrick and I would start talking about our spouses and our kids, and it was wonderful. He was very kind and very real. In fact, we got along so well that Kevin even wrote in an extra scene for the two of us that we shot on the Disney lot in LA a few weeks later.

And do you know what? As mortified as I was, I think Patrick kind of liked the fact that I had no idea who he was. It had to be exhausting having fans gawking at him all the time. Listening to me chatter on endlessly about Georgia, homeschooling, and the joys of country living was probably a welcome break. After all, dear, what is idle prattle for?

Now Amy Adams, *Enchanted*'s Princess Giselle, I *did* know. She is an amazing actress and had actually done quite a bit of musical theatre growing up, so we hit it off instantly. Amy is a huge *Mermaid* fan, and she was a little nervous because Alan Menken had also done the music for *Enchanted*, and she was afraid she wouldn't be able to do his songs justice. I told her, "Listen. You're going to be great, sweetie. Don't worry about it. Just enjoy yourself, live in the moment, and have fun."

~~~~~~~~~

If only I listened to my own advice every once in a while. But then again, I rarely know what I'm doing.

Take homeschooling. I didn't know how to do that either. God knows, it was never part of the plan. In fact, before we left California, Ray and I jumped through about a dozen hoops to get McKinley into this unbelievably competitive preschool in LA. Seriously, you have no idea. Parents practically have to put their child's name on the list the day they conceive, and even then there are no guarantees.

But McKinley was off-the-charts intelligent. He was reading by the time he was two (in fairness, some of it might have been memorization since Ray and I read to him constantly). He had been coming to work with me since he was 2 weeks old, and by the time he was 18 months old, he could name all the instruments in the orchestra. He knew composers. He knew styles of music. He just soaked it all up like a sponge.

We began taking him to the Guitar Center in Los Angeles

once a week after piano class, and we would go upstairs where all the super expensive drum kits were. He would plop himself down and play for 15 minutes straight. It was crazy. Professional musicians would just sit and watch him in amazement. Of course, he could barely reach the pedals. Still, the kid was a whiz.

Within two months of attending this ultra exclusive preschool, though, McKinley started to regress. All of a sudden, he started using baby talk, and whenever I dropped him off at school, he would latch onto me and refuse to let go. Then he'd start sobbing. It was horrific. The headmistress kept insisting that it was "perfectly normal," but for *my* kid it wasn't.

One day I walked him into school, and as soon as I let go of his hand, he started crying, "Please don't leave me here! I want to go home with you!"

I knelt down in front of him to try to calm him down, and as soon as I reached his eye level, he pulled himself together and in his most grown-up voice said, "If you promise me this is the last day I have to be here, then I'll make it."

And now my heart was torn in two.

"Buddy," I said, "I promise you, today's your last day."

As soon as I got him settled on the playground, I walked straight into the headmistress's office and politely but firmly announced, "Today will be McKinley's last day."

She looked at me as though I had sprouted a second head. "What are you planning to do?"

"I'm going to homeschool him," I said defiantly.

She just shook her head. "You're making the biggest mistake of his life. He's going to fall behind, he's going to lose his place in line . . ."

"We'll see," I said. Then I marched back out to the playground, picked up McKinley, and said, "Come on, buddy. We're leaving."

It wasn't until I got to the car that I realized I *really* hadn't thought this through. *I don't know how to homeschool. I'm not a teacher. I'm working full-time. I'm on the road twice a month. I've got an infant at home. Oh gosh, what have I done?*

Then I looked in the rearview mirror and saw McKinley's little tearstained face smiling back at me from his car seat and thought, *I may not know what I'm doing . . . but I'm glad I'm doing it.*

Later that afternoon, McKinley and I went to one of those school-supply stores that teachers use. I filled our basket with everything that looked age-appropriate for McKinley, and when we got home, I set up a little table and chairs in front of the big bay window in our bedroom and just . . . made school.

The original plan was to finish preschool at home (surely I could handle that) and then enroll him in kindergarten somewhere the following semester. But when the time came, McKinley was adamant. "I don't want to go anywhere else. I want to do school here with you." So we did. Then two years later, we added Delaney into the mix.

By the time McKinley was six and Delaney was four, we were living in Georgia. Once again, my intention was to stop homeschooling and enroll McKinley in a private Christian school. Funny thing is, for someone who had no idea what she was doing, it turns out we had done a pretty good job. In fact, when McKinley was tested, we discovered he was a good one to two grades ahead of other kids his age. And Delaney was such a quick learner, with a photographic memory and unbelievably strong spatial skills, that she breezed through her curriculum and jumped one to two grade levels in most of her subjects. Unfortunately, the school was not set up to accommodate that, and we didn't want them to be two full years younger than everyone else in their classes, so Ray and I converted our upstairs sunroom into a classroom, and the next thing we knew, we were officially a homeschooling family.

We weren't legalistic about it. We gave McKinley and Delaney the choice at the end of every semester as to whether they wanted to keep working with me at home or go to a traditional school. Every time, without fail, they both opted to stick with me. Clearly they had a lot more confidence in me than I had.

It wasn't so bad when they were little, but once we started getting into biology, chemistry, algebra, and world history, there were some pretty rough days. A lot of times I'd get them both set up with something (and bear in mind, they were two and a half years apart, so we had two different curriculums going on at the same time) and tell them, "I'll be back in 10 minutes." Then I'd go into my little closet, close the door, and have a big old fat cry. I just felt so utterly and completely unqualified. I was 100 percent convinced I was ruining both of their lives.

Sometimes I'd wander into Ray's office and break down; to his credit, he always knew the right thing to say. He'd remind me, "You know what, sweetie? You love those kids. That's all they need. God will provide everything else. All you can do is take it one day at a time, keep putting one foot in front of the other, and pray."

I spent a lot of time in prayer that season. I also spent a lot of time in that closet. I would literally get down on my face and say, "Jesus, I do not understand this concept. Please help me learn this. Show me where to reach out. Help me find the help and support I need."

Truth be told, that was the hardest part. There really weren't any other moms doing what I was doing. Homeschooling, yes. But homeschooling while working full-time in the entertainment industry, while traveling anywhere from 25 to 35 times a year? Nope.

The other homeschool moms I had gotten to know were all very supportive, and we did a lot of fun things together—outings, field trips, craft days—but we just had very different lives. And that felt very isolating.

Of course, I wasn't alone. One homeschooling friend, Daryl Waite, understood my loneliness, and she loved and encouraged me through it. Ray was also a huge help. When I was home, I would do all the teaching and Ray would keep the ship afloat, taking care of groceries, meals, laundry, cleaning, bills, all of that. And whenever I had to travel for work by myself, Ray would take over homeschooling duties. When we traveled as a family, we would just pack up all our school stuff, and Ray would teach the kids out of a hotel, a concert hall, a cruise ship, or wherever we happened to be.

In that sense, our kids kind of got the best of everything. I mean, they got a ton of one-on-one time with both of us, plus they got to travel, meet new people, see new places, and experience different countries and cultures. How many kids get to do that?

People used to say to me, "Oh, those poor kids. They're going to be so antisocial." But nothing could be further from the truth. Not only are they both incredibly social, they're also comfortable in intergenerational settings. They can talk to anybody, anywhere, in any part of the world. It doesn't matter.

There is no such thing as a stranger to my kids. Plus they've done church camps, youth groups, mission trips, soccer leagues—they have a fantastic network of friends. And by the time they got to high school, they were each attending traditional school for a few hours every day—McKinley for TV/film/AV production and Delaney for musical theatre, acting, and music. In fact, by the time she graduated, Delaney had 24 shows on her résumé and had been accepted to her dream school, the University of Cincinnati College-Conservatory of Music (CCM), which had been my dream school as well. That's not antisocial at all.

Mostly, though, people would tell me, "You homeschool? Oh, I could *never* do that."

And my answer to them was always, "Yes, you could. If I can do it, anybody can do it. All you have to do is love your kid. That's it. God will take care of the rest."

They never believed me. "Oh, my gosh," they'd say. "We would drive each other crazy."

You know what? I thought the same thing when I started, but the truth is, homeschooling has strengthened my relationship with my kids more than I ever would have thought possible. I think that's been the biggest surprise, really. It's fascinating—when you pour into someone, it comes back to you tenfold.

And it's not just me. Delaney and McKinley are in their twenties now, and they're still extremely close; that never would have happened if we hadn't spent so much time traveling, learning, and just plain doing life together. Sometimes they'll set aside an entire evening just to hang out, watch movies, play board games, and have fun; and no one is invited—not even Ray and I. And it's such a comfort to Ray and me because we can rest knowing that long after we're gone, the kids will still have each other, and that their bond will be stronger than it *ever* would have been if they hadn't spent so much time together growing up.

Sometimes people will comment to Ray and me, "You two have really raised amazing kids," and we always say, "Thank you, but it wasn't us. God did that. We were just blessed to be their parents and get to walk alongside them on the journey."

I give *all* the credit to God for the way our kids turned out. He's the only reason I was able to make it through almost 16 years of homeschooling between our two kids. I wasn't qualified. I didn't ask to homeschool my kids, and initially I didn't even want to. It just sort of happened. I saw my kid struggling, and the words came out. That wasn't my will. That was His.

Over the years, I've learned that if God really wants me to do something, He will give me the courage, the strength, the endurance, the patience, and the ability to do it—and do it well.

All I have to bring to the table is an open mind, an open heart, a willingness to try, and an obedient spirit. He'll do the rest. God's pretty awesome that way. And thank goodness He is, because I rarely know what I'm doing. I didn't know what I was doing when I stood behind a mic for the first time. I didn't know what I was doing when I stood in front of a camera for the first time. And I definitely didn't know what I was doing when I boldly declared to the headmistress, "I'm going to homeschool him." But, *wow*, am I ever glad I did. God can do extraordinary things through very ordinary people. I'm living proof of that.

23

~~~~~~

"My One and Only"

There was a time when all I cared about was getting my Equity card, moving from ensemble to lead, and seeing my name up in lights. Now all I want to do is finish my work as quickly and efficiently as possible so I can get home, put on my pajamas, and hang out with my family.

Life has a way of shifting your priorities. When you're single, you're focused primarily on you. Then you add a spouse, and your focus is split. Add in a few kids, and suddenly your life is no longer as much about you as it is about them. And that's good. In fact, it's amazing.

After the kids were born, I turned down all kinds of jobs that I would have leapt at in my twenties, and I don't regret saying no to a single one of them. Life is just too fragile and too precious to risk missing out on once-in-a-lifetime moments with McKinley and Delaney just so I can add one more line to my résumé.

A few years ago, I had an opportunity to audition for the national touring production of *Dear Evan Hansen*. I loved the music, and I loved the part. But Delaney was in her senior year of high school, and I didn't want to miss it. In fact, that's the litmus test Ray and I would use whenever a job offer came in while the kids were growing up. He would say to me, "Let's say you take this job and end up missing McKinley's birthday or Delaney's recital. Would you be able to live with yourself?" No, I wouldn't. It just wasn't worth it. The moment I set my priorities as God first, then family, then work, the decision-making process pretty much took care of itself.

I absolutely treasure my kids and my husband. They mean more to me than anything in the world. And there's nothing I wouldn't do or give up for them.

There is a verse in the Gospel of Matthew that says, "Where your treasure is, there your heart will be also."[1] Never did that message ring truer for me than in January 2020.

Ray and I were getting ready to go on a weeklong trip to Maui. I had a concert scheduled with a local symphony there, and since neither of us had ever been before, we thought, *Why not extend the trip a few days and make a vacation out of it?* McKinley and Delaney were both away at college, so it was going to be our first empty nester vacation. We had all kinds of fun activities planned: hiking, climbing up the side of a volcano, horseback riding on the beach—the works.

Two days before we were scheduled to leave, Ray went in for a routine physical. There was nothing wrong with him. He didn't have any symptoms, and he was in great shape.

In fact, he was biking 15 to 20 miles a day. But when he came home, he had a weird expression on his face.

"What's the matter?" I asked.

"Well," he said, "I had some blood work done back in November—nothing fancy, just the usual stuff. But they did some more extensive tests today, and the doctor has some concerns."

I didn't like the sound of that. "What do you mean—*concerns?*"

"He didn't like the look of certain numbers that came back."

"So . . . what does he want to do?"

"It's got something to do with my heart and blood flow, and he said there's a chance he could be wrong, but just to be sure, he wants to do a heart catheterization."

I liked the sound of that even less. "What is that, exactly?"

Ray assured me it was just an outpatient procedure, which made it sound slightly less frightening. But still.

"Is it risky?"

"No, I don't think so. But it's invasive." I was trying to wrap my mind around that when Ray said, "He said I can still go on the trip. In fact, he said I could even go on that ski trip with the guys in a few weeks."

Wait . . . what? "So the doctor said, 'Go ahead with these two things, and *then* come in and do the test'?"

"Well . . . yeah."

"Why would he do that?"

"I told him I was kind of busy and asked if it could wait. He said—"

"Whoa, whoa, whoa. Wait a minute." This was not making sense to me at all. "If this is a blockage thing, and it has to do with your heart, do you think we should be going all the way to Hawaii? I mean, what if something were to happen? *Is* something going to happen?"

"No," he said. "Nothing's going to happen. I feel great. I don't even have any symptoms. I'm sure it's nothing."

Normally, I trust Ray's gut 100 percent, but for some reason, this time I just felt the Holy Spirit prompting me to hit pause.

"Yeah, but, Ray, if these tests have come back and there are question marks on them that have to do with your heart, don't you think maybe you should get it checked out first and *then* start traveling cross-country, climbing volcanoes, and skiing in the mountains?"

By the way, remember when I said Ray tends to be super analytical and I am more of a fly-by-the-seat-of-your-pants kind of gal? Have you noticed how that went right out the window here? We call that keeping the magic alive.

"You know what? Maybe I should call the doctor back," he finally conceded.

"Honey, I *really* think you should." As I sat there at the kitchen table listening to Ray talk to his doctor, I could not for the life of me figure out what would possess him to take that kind of risk with his health. I mean, what's a trip to Hawaii when we're talking about a potential heart problem?

He turned and looked at me. "He said they can do it in two days."

"Then we're doing it," I said.

He just stared at me, the phone muffled against his chest. "But what about your concert? You can't miss that."

That's what's bothering him?

"Don't worry about that," I told him. "Take the appointment. I'll figure something out."

"Are you sure?"

"Absolutely." There was no question in my mind about that. Concerts come and go. I've done so many of them over the past 30 years, and God willing, I'll get to do a lot more. But I have only one husband. And McKinley and Delaney have only one dad. There was no way I was going to risk Ray's health over a one-night-only event and a week at the beach.

As soon as we had Ray's procedure confirmed, we called the kids. Of course, they both were extremely upset and wanted to come home right away. We said no. McKinley was in the final days of filming his senior-thesis short film at the Savannah College of Art and Design (SCAD), and Delaney was in the middle of rehearsing her freshman showcase at CCM, so the timing was terrible for both of them. Besides, my cousin Robin and my friend Angela would both be coming to the hospital with me, so it wasn't as though I would be alone.

"Let's just find out what's going on," I told them. "It could very well be nothing. We just wanted you to know what is happening. I promise I'll call you the second I know anything."

"Are you sure there isn't anything we can do?" they asked. Actually, there was.

"Pray."

~~~~~~~~

Two days later, I took Ray in to the hospital. They told me the entire procedure should last about an hour, so after they wheeled Ray off, I settled into the waiting room with Robin and Angela. Not 30 minutes later, a young woman in scrubs walked in and called, "Benson?"

"Yep. Right here."

She was all smiles. "He's all done."

Wow, that was fast.

"He's in recovery now if you'd like to go back and see him."

"Absolutely!" I grabbed my purse and followed her through the door.

"He's doing great!" she said.

I was thrilled. Obviously, they hadn't found anything. How else could they have finished so quickly?

When I got to the recovery room, I said a quick hello to the nurse, then leaned over the gurney where Ray was lying.

"Hey, sweetie," I said, smiling. "I can't believe how fast that went. You're like Superman!"

That's when I noticed he had tears streaming down the sides of his face. I glanced up at the nurse. She was just quietly shaking her head.

"What's wrong?" I asked.

Before either of them could say anything, the doctor came in. They had found six severe blockages in Ray's arteries—a 99 percent blockage in his right main artery and a 60 to 70 percent blockage in the remaining five.

I had no words. I just held Ray's hand and stared blankly at the images of his heart on the screen.

"It's probably been slowly developing over the past decade," the doctor said.

"But he hasn't had any symptoms. In fact, he just did a 105-mile bike ride, climbing 11,000 vertical feet—in

92-degree heat! How is that even possible if all of his arteries are blocked?"

As ridiculous as it sounds, part of me half expected him to say, "You know what? You're right. This is the wrong scan." Instead he pulled out his pen and pointed to a barely visible curvy line on the screen.

"Do you see this little vein, right here? This is what's been keeping you alive, Ray. This little vein is pumping blood to your heart once every five beats." He put his pen back in his pocket, looked at the screen, and shook his head. "It's really quite miraculous."

I squinted at the screen to get a better look. There it was: one teeny, almost threadlike vein looping all the way down and around Ray's heart. That's what Ray was living on. That's what he was riding on. A tiny bypass that God had created to keep him going.

At that moment, everything about our lives changed. I saw the fear in Ray's eyes and squeezed his hand a little tighter.

"Everything's going to be fine, honey," I assured him. "We're going to get through this. We're going to take it one step at a time."

I stayed with him for a few more minutes, but he was so groggy from the anesthesia, he could barely keep his eyes open. When he laid his head back down to rest, I stepped out into the hall, closed the door behind me, and just lost it.

Okay, I said to myself. *This is not the news we anticipated, but I'm going to choose to see the positives in this. Yes, there is a lot of blockage, but look what God did. He not only found a way to keep Ray's heart beating but also brought the problem to our attention before the damage was irreversible. And if He can do all of that, He can get us through the rest of this.*

Then I got to work. I had asked the doctor to forward all of Ray's results to Dr. Mark Leimbach. Mark was not only a fantastic cardiologist but also a dear friend and neighbor. I trusted him completely. So I found a quiet spot in the hall, plopped down on the floor, and got him on the phone.

"Okay, Mark, talk me through this," I said.

"Hang on," he said, "I'm looking at the findings right now." Mark basically confirmed everything the other doctor had said. He also said that Ray was going to need bypass surgery.

"If it were you, who would you want to do your surgery?" I asked him.

"Well, we still don't know how many bypasses they're going to have to do. It could be two, three, maybe even four or five. But Dan Winston's the only guy I would ever let operate on me."

"Okay," I said, scribbling Dan's name down. "Who else do we need?"

"The only anesthesiologist Dan works with is Rick Trent. That'd be your A-team."

We knew Rick too. Like Mark, he was a neighbor of ours. I was starting to feel a glimmer of hope. God's hand just seemed to be everywhere in this.

"I'll call Dan and see if I can get you guys an appointment with him sometime later this week."

"Oh no," I interrupted him, "we are *not* leaving this hospital. We're staying put until the surgery."

"Jodi, he can't stay. This was an outpatient procedure. It's not an emergency."

He had to be joking. "Mark, all of Ray's arteries are severely blocked. Don't tell me they're going to send us home."

"I'm afraid so. Ray didn't have a heart attack or a stroke, so technically the bypass surgery is elective."

Is he serious?

"Bear in mind, Jodi, Ray's probably been living like this for years. He'll be fine until we can get him in to see Dan. Nothing is going to happen."

I hoped he was right.

Later that afternoon, after I got Ray home and settled into bed, I called the kids. Of course, they were both incredibly upset.

"Look," I said, "I know this is really scary, but think about what God has already done. We found out about the problem before anything bad happened, Dr. Leimbach is getting us an appointment with a top-notch cardiothoracic surgeon, your dad's going to get a brand-new heart, and he's going to be better than ever."

I knew what was coming next: "We want to be there for the surgery."

"Absolutely. You guys need to be here with your dad in pre-op, you need to be here when he rolls out, and you need to be here when he wakes up." They were both still very upset. I can handle a lot of things, but hearing my kids cry? That's just the worst.

I remember once, when Delaney was four years old, we were all having breakfast together, and she was singing between bites, using her Little Mermaid fork like a conductor's baton. All of a sudden, the fork jolted toward her right eye. She screamed, and my heart sank. Before I could even move, she covered her eye with her hand and started wailing.

I quickly scooped her up, and the four of us hurried out to the van. I did my best to calm her down, gently pressing a small towel to her eye to keep it shut while Ray raced us to the hospital at breakneck speed with the flashers on. I was sitting on the floor between the kids' seats in the back, trying my best to keep everyone calm by doing the only thing I could think of—praying. And I'm not talking about silent, gentle, contemplative praying. I was full-on crying out to God for help, as were McKinley and Ray. At one point, I gently lifted the towel to take a quick look at Delaney's eye. It was a milky-gray color, and I couldn't see the pupil. It was as if her eye had lost all signs of life. I felt physically sick.

"I can't see anything, Mommy!" she cried out.

"It's okay, sweetie," I assured her. "It's okay. You're gonna be okay." I quickly wiped the tears off her cheeks with the edge of the towel and covered her eye back up. With tears streaming down my own face, I continued to pray out loud with Ray and McKinley. By the time we got to the hospital, Delaney was in complete shock, and Ray, McKinley, and I were near hysterics. It was absolutely terrifying.

Within minutes of checking into the emergency room, we met with a pediatric ophthalmologist. She was very kind and soft-spoken. As she began examining Delaney, I quietly took a step back and turned away. I couldn't look. Ray and McKinley's eyes were glued to the doctor's back, their lips frantically mouthing prayers. I don't think any of us had stopped praying since we left the house.

After she had thoroughly examined Delaney's eye, the doctor turned to us and asked what happened. When I told her about the fork hitting Delaney's eye, she looked at me quizzically and said, "That's really strange. I don't see any abrasions. Not even a scratch. In fact, I see absolutely no evidence whatsoever of any impact to her eye."

I took a few steps forward and looked at Delaney's eye. I couldn't believe it. The lifeless, milky-gray image that I had fully expected to haunt my dreams for years was gone. Delaney's eye was as bright, sparkling, and blue as ever.

It was a miracle. An absolute miracle. And a great reminder that no matter what happens, we have to trust that God is still God and knows best. If God could work a miracle for Delaney, I believed He could also work one for Ray.

Before we hung up, I let each of the kids talk with Ray for a few minutes, which I think did wonders for all of them, and I told them I would call as soon as we had a date set for the surgery.

And what a date it was.

~~~~~~~~~

"So, Ray, how does a new heart on Valentine's Day sound?"

Ray and I looked at each other, then back at Dr. Winston. "Are you serious?" I asked.

"Yep," he said. "It's my day off, and Rick Trent is on vacation that day, but if that date works for you, we'd be happy to come in. So what do you think? Does Valentine's Day sound like a good day?"

I grabbed Ray's hand. "It sounds like a perfect day."

Ray spent the next three weeks fitted with a heart monitor and on virtual bed rest—no cycling, no stairs, no sports on TV—nothing that might raise his heart rate at all. For 21 straight days, I kept that house as calm and as quiet as a tomb. That, by the way, was so not us. We are a *very* musical family, and Ray and I are both pretty social, so it's not often you can hear a pin drop in the Benson house, especially when all four of us are there. Sadly, there was a brief five-day stretch when even I wasn't there. I had a concert at Walt Disney World, and no matter how hard I tried, I could *not* get out of it. I hated, hated, *hated* the idea of leaving Ray. Fortunately, our niece Ashley graciously agreed to come down and take care of her uncle while I was gone. She also planned to be with us on the day of Ray's surgery, which was an enormous blessing.

The morning of the 14th, we checked in to the hospital at 5 a.m. sharp. Ray was the first and only surgery on the docket for Dr. Winston and his team, and I got to talk to every one of them before they took him in. I gave each one a big hug, thanked them for everything they were doing, and made sure they knew we were going to be praying for them throughout the entire surgery. It was such a blessing to get to say those things to everybody before Ray was wheeled away. And when he was—wow, that was hard.

Ray was understandably upset, so the kids and I started cracking little jokes to try to cheer him up: "Don't go toward the light, Dad. Turn away from the light." "If you go to heaven, sweetie, say hi to your mom and dad for me." "I hope you have an amazing trip . . . but make sure you come back." What can I say? We're weird.

After they wheeled Ray into surgery, Ashley, the kids, and I hunkered down in the waiting room. It was still early, and we were the only ones there, which was a relief, because as soon as I sat down, I started to cry.

"I'm fine," I assured the kids between sobs. "I just need to let this out, but I'm good. I promise. I'm good." Honestly, as much as it probably freaked out the kids, those tears were very healing, I think. This cry had been a good three weeks in the making.

The next four hours were a waiting game. One by one, our loving family and friends started to fill the waiting room. All of them came with food and drinks, ready to wait and pray with us. I can't tell you how loved our family felt. It was overwhelming.

Every once in a while, the nurse would call my cell or the phone in the waiting room to let me know what was happening—"They've removed the vein from the leg; they thought they found a leaky valve, but it ended up being okay"—and of course the big one—"He's off the heart and lung machine." The staff was extremely informative, and I really appreciated that.

Sometime around noon, we received word that the surgery was over and it had been a success. All told, they ended up doing five bypasses. Five. That's still hard for me to wrap my head around.

We were allowed to go back and see Ray for a few minutes. He was still intubated and under anesthesia, but just being able to see him and knowing we were finally on the other side of this felt wonderful.

When Dr. Winston came to talk to me, I hugged him and thanked him profusely. "How do you feel about it?" I asked through tears of joy. "Did everything go like you'd hoped?"

"I'm not trying to pump myself up or anything," he said, "but I really feel like we did an amazing job. We didn't know until we got in there whether it was going to be two, three, four, or five, but I went with five because I felt like it was the best choice for Ray; we had a good vein to work with, and we felt confident that we could do it. So everything in there is all cleaned up, cleaned out, and good as new."

I was overwhelmed with gratitude. I gave Dr. Winston one final hug and exhaled for the first time since January. I was utterly exhausted but indescribably happy.

My valentine had a brand-new heart. Praise God.

A few hours later, after Ray was awake, we got to go back and talk with him. He was pretty loopy, but the kids didn't care. Just being able to see their dad's face and make eye contact with him was enough to set their hearts and minds at ease.

At around 5:30, I asked Ashley to drive the kids home and make sure they got something to eat and some rest. We had been up since 4 a.m., and they were both exhausted. I stayed the night at the hospital. They had a little hotel room on the ICU floor, so I sat with Ray until about 11 p.m. When the night shift took over, I made sure all the nurses had my cell number and knew where I was. Then I went to my little room, took a shower, slipped into my pajamas, and collapsed into bed. And do you know what? It was, without question, the best Valentine's Day I have ever had.

~~~~~~

Ray stayed in the hospital for five days. And I cannot tell you how overwhelmed I was by the support we received. We had so many friends come by to visit, some of whom called in advance to let us know they were coming and others who just showed up.

One of our sweet friends, Donna Reeves, who had lost her husband to cancer not long before, texted me: "I'd like to come by and drop off a little care bag. I know what it's like to live in a hospital." God bless her, she brought us a warm, cozy, fuzzy blanket that Ray and I both loved and used, and extra bottles of water and snacks so I didn't have to keep going to the nurse's station and asking, "May I please have another this and another that?" It was just really thoughtful. But that wasn't all. Donna is also a licensed massage therapist, and when Ray was still in the ICU, she got permission to come up and give him a 30-minute massage. I offered to pay her, but she wouldn't hear of it.

"I just really want to do this for Ray," she said. "His body's been through World War III. I did the same thing for my husband, and it was really helpful."

I never would have thought of that. What an incredible blessing to have friends like Donna.

Once we got home, the ladies in my small group brought meals over to the house every other night, which was huge, because as you'll recall, I'm not much of a cook. And of course, our neighbors would stop by several times a week just to ask, "What do you need? Can we pick anything up for you at the store? How can we help?"

For weeks, there was a steady stream of visitors in and out of the house—mostly Ray's biking buddies, but a lot of my girlfriends came by as well to make sure I felt loved and cared for. Even friends and family from out of state called and texted to let us know they were thinking about us and praying for us.

I shouldn't have been surprised; we'd been surrounded with love and support from the start of our ordeal. The day Ray had his cath procedure, our dear friends from Florida, John and Christina, showed up in the waiting room. I had texted them the night before to let them know what was going on, but I never expected them to come. I mean, for an *outpatient* procedure? Who does that? It turns out they were in Georgia looking at wedding venues for their oldest son, and when they got my text asking for prayer, they decided to take a little detour. Because as Christina had said, "That's what friends do." And Ray and I have been blessed to have some of the best.

By the way, that concert in Maui Ray was so worried about me missing? My agent ended up finding another vocalist who was able to step in and do the exact same song list I had sent to the symphony a few weeks earlier. What's more, she was able to bring her husband with her and turn it into a little vacation, just like Ray and I had planned to do. So the whole last-minute cancellation turned out to be just as big a blessing for them as it was for us.

As I write this, Ray and his brand-new heart just celebrated their second anniversary. He's back on his bike, and he's as healthy as ever. He and his buddies even got to go on that ski trip they had to reschedule.

As for our trip to Maui . . . well, like everything else in our lives, we're leaving that up to God. If we get to go someday, great. And if we don't, that's fine too. It honestly doesn't matter. I already have everything my heart could ever desire.

24

John 15:5

I love my job.

Gosh, how I love my job.

Trying to imagine my life without Disney or Ariel is almost like trying to imagine my life without Ray and the kids: It's impossible. Being Ariel isn't just my job; it's also my ministry. It's the way I get to connect with and love on people.

It's been more than 30 years since *The Little Mermaid*, and people still tell me how much it means to them. Whenever I'm at a convention or a meet and greet, I always keep a box of Kleenex at my table because the emotions the movie triggers are so strong. For some, it rekindles memories of a beloved parent or grandparent with whom they saw the movie but who is no longer with them. For others, it simply reminds them of happier times, before life got painful, complicated, and hard. Over the years, God has used Ariel to provide comfort to children who can't walk or speak, and He's used her to give people who suffer with depression hope that there's a way out of the darkness.

I've met thousands of people over the years whose lives have been impacted by *Mermaid*, and the fact that I got to play even the tiniest part has been one of the greatest blessings of my life. So when I got an unexpected call in 2011 from Chris Montan, the president of Walt Disney Music, I was a little nervous. For one thing, Chris had never called me before. In addition, there had been quite a few casting changes in the character-voice department that year, especially to some of the classic princesses. It happens more than you might think. Sometimes the original voice actor passes away or retires, and sometimes people's voices change over time, so they no longer sound recognizable as that character. Over the years, there have been multiple voices lent to Snow White, Sleeping Beauty, and Cinderella, as well as several other Disney characters. Even Mickey Mouse is currently on his fourth. The changes are rarely, if ever, advertised because ultimately, the character comes first, and the goal of Disney Character Voices (DCV) is to maintain as much consistency and integrity as possible. That's part of what makes the characters so timeless. Mickey Mouse sounds the same today as he did when Walt was his first voice back in the 1920s. So if the powers that be had decided it was time for me to step aside and let someone else become Ariel, then, well, it had been a great ride.

Chris and I gave each other quick updates on our lives and asked about each other's families—the usual chitchat. Finally I couldn't take it anymore.

"Listen, Chris, I just want you to know that I've really, *really* appreciated all these years with the company. It's been an amazing ride, and I've had a wonderful time. So whatever you decide, it's all good, really."

"What are you talking about?"

"Well, it's just that I know there have been a lot of transitions over at DCV lately, and I totally understand if you guys think it's time for someone else to step in and—"

"Jodi," he broke in, "I was just calling to see if you'd be able to fly out to Los Angeles in August. We'd like to honor you by making you a Disney Legend."

I literally dropped the phone.

"Jodi? Are you there?"

I picked the phone back up and blurted out, "Oh, my gosh. I'm so sorry. I thought you were letting me go."

"What?" He laughed out loud. "Why would we do that?"

"I don't . . . Really? Legend?" My head was spinning. "I thought . . . don't you have to be dead to get that?" Since the Disney Legend was Disney's version of a lifetime achievement award, I had always assumed it went only to people who had either passed away or were at the very end of their illustrious careers.

"No, you're *all* alive," he assured me.

Five princesses were inducted that year: me; Paige; Lea Salonga, who was the singing voice of Mulan and Jasmine; Linda Larkin, the speaking voice of Jasmine; and Anika Noni Rose, who played Tiana in *The Princess and the Frog.* And we were all very much alive. Still . . . *why me?*

Most of the people I knew who had gotten a Legend Award had been with the company forever. So many had been with Disney far longer than I had and were far more deserving—all those wonderful unsung heroes quietly work-ing behind the scenes for years, making it happen with no spotlight and no applause.

I mean, it's always nice to have your work recognized, but that's not why I got into this. I've never really given much thought to awards or accolades, and I typically do press or publicity only when the company asks me to. To be honest, the thought of *me* getting this award was a little embarrass-ing, but *wow*, what an enormous honor.

You'd think that with months to prepare, by the day of the ceremony I'd have drafted dozens of acceptance speeches and spent hours practicing in front of a mirror—but no. There I was standing backstage at the Anaheim Convention Center, dressed to the hilt, clutching a tiny scrap of paper with a list of names I had jotted down at the last minute. There hadn't even been any method or madness to creating that list; I'd just jotted down whomever God brought to mind. But the more I looked at the list, the more names kept popping into my head. I mean, it *had been* 26 years. How many people had touched or spoken into my life in 26 years? I was terrified I was going to forget someone.

"Once you get to the podium," the stage manager whis-pered, "you'll have 60 seconds to give your speech."

Sixty seconds? Wow.

"Okay, I'm just going to apologize right now, because I have a lot of people to thank, and I don't want to leave any-body out. I mean, I'll do my best, but I'm probably gonna run over a little."

She just waved me off. "Oh, Jodi, don't worry about it. You'll be fine. It's not like we're televised and have to break for a commercial or something. Just take your time and have fun."

Now, I've spent the better part of my life onstage—singing, dancing, schmoozing with the audience—and I've got to tell you, standing behind that little podium . . . I had never been so nervous. How do you sum up 26 years' worth of blessings in under a minute? And yet I knew exactly where I wanted to start.

"Praise God from whom all blessings flow that I'm standing here today."

Then I held up my little Disney cast member ID card. "I'm a proud cast member of our Disney company. This card is 26 years old. It doesn't swipe anymore. I couldn't get my discount yesterday."

For the record, that little magnetic strip hasn't worked for years. Not as if that stops me from whipping it out and trying every time we go to the parks. It drives Ray and the kids crazy. In fact, we've had a running joke about it for as long as I can remember.

"I'm very, very proud of this card," I continued. "I'm very proud of the Walt Disney Company. It's my family. I'm blessed beyond belief. It is because of all of you out there that I get to be here today."

I really did want to honor the other cast members. After all, we're a team. They're all amazing, and if I could have named every last one of them in the 60 seconds I was allotted, I would have in a heartbeat.

Of course, there were a few people I did name personally: Ray, McKinley and Delaney, my mom, and Roy Disney, who sadly had passed away just two years earlier. Gosh, how I wish he could have been there. And of course, Howard. How could I not thank Howard? He was the reason I was there in the first place, as were Alan, Ron Clements and John Musker,

Glen and Linda Keane, Chris Montan, Rick Dempsey, and the entire team at Disney Character Voices. I knew I had left names out, probably dozens of them. I could only hope and pray they all knew how much they meant to me, and that without them, I would never have been there.

There was only one other person I wanted to thank before I left that stage, and one thing I wanted to make sure everybody in that room heard me say loud and clear, and it was this: "This is not a job. This is a gift that God has given me. John 15:5 is my life verse: 'I am the vine; you are the branches. If you remain in me and I in you, you will bear much fruit; apart from me you can do nothing.'[1] I can do nothing without my God."

I love that verse. I love the truth of that verse. Apart from God, I can do absolutely nothing. Every accomplishment I've ever had and every accolade I've ever received belongs to Him. From the very beginning, He has been my producer, my director, my choreographer, my voice coach—my everything.

I could not have planned or predicted anything that has happened to me. Nor could I have made any of it happen on my own. It was all God's unique design for my life, and when I look back over my journey, I can see His hand at work in every step of it, nudging me in the right direction and putting just the right people in my path at just the right moments. None of it was visible to me, of course—at least not at the time. But now I can see how He led me so clearly.

The best way I can think to describe His guidance in my life is that it's like counted cross-stitch. I never had the patience for cross-stitch growing up, but my mom and sister used to do it all the time. I was always so fascinated by it because when I looked on the back side of each piece, I just saw a big bunch of knots, zigzags, and threads going every which way. But when I turned it over, it looked beautiful—this amazingly intricate design. I used to marvel at their pieces and think, *How did they do that? How did they take something so messy and make something so beautiful?*

That's a picture of what God's done with my life.

He took all the knots, sharp turns, and frayed ends—my early marriage struggles, miscarriages, and career setbacks—and somehow made them all into something beautiful. And for me, the Legend ceremony was a celebration of that. It was my opportunity to say thank you to all the people who had been part of my journey and to give credit where credit was due. Because make no mistake: I was not responsible for any of it. And even though I'm not comfortable with accolades and awards, becoming a Legend really mattered to me, because Ariel mattered to me and Disney mattered to me. They still do—more than you can imagine.

Becoming a Disney Legend makes you an ambassador for the Walt Disney Company, and I take that role very seriously. It means a lot to me to represent our company. It means a lot to all of us.

When the kids were little and we would go to the Disney parks, I always explained to them, "This is a really lovely gift and a lovely opportunity, and we need to represent our family and Disney well. When people stop us along the way, we need to be kind and patient." Granted, sometimes when Delaney and McKinley were small, they'd get a little fussy while they waited for me to stop for pictures or to talk to little ones on our way to a ride, but for the most part, they were (and are) great about it. In fact, they usually notice

Mermaid fans before I do. They're constantly tapping me on the arm and saying, "Mom, there's somebody waiting for a photo over there" or "There's a little girl heading over on your left." It's like they have radar or something.

And we do get stopped a lot because I don't go incognito—no dark sunglasses or hair pulled back and stuffed under a hat. In fact, the parks are the only place I feel comfortable wearing an Ariel T-shirt. I don't wear one anywhere else because that would feel too self-promotional and weird. I do wear a Mickey Mouse sweatshirt around at home—it's a little more universal, so I can get away with it. But when I'm at one of the parks, I wear a different Ariel T-shirt every day. I even go all out and borrow Delaney's little Ariel ears. And why not? It's the one place you get to dress up, have fun, and be a kid again. Besides, it's my job to represent the merfolk, and I love doing it. I love every part of being Ariel.

~~~~~~~~~

Without question, one of the biggest blessings of my job— and the part that gives me an incredible amount of joy—is when I get to serve as a guest narrator for the Candlelight Processional—a Christmas celebration that Disney hosts every year from the day after Thanksgiving through December 30. The event takes place at Epcot in the American Gardens outdoor theatre, and it is spectacular. There's a 50-piece orchestra and a choir of Disney cast members arranged vertically in the form of a Christmas tree. On either side of them stands a high school choir. Choirs come in from all over the country to perform—a different one every night, and they raise their own funds to do it. The Candlelight Processional is one of Disney's most popular events, and it's packed to the gills every night.

As the narrator, I get to read the Christmas story from the book of Luke, which is so incredibly powerful. The whole evening is filled with Scripture, with carols like "O Come All Ye Faithful," "Silent Night," and "Joy to the World" woven in throughout. It all builds to an unbelievably beautiful rendition of Handel's "Hallelujah Chorus." I always sing along. I don't know if I'm supposed to, but good luck stopping me. I've done it so many times now that the stage crew pretty much leaves my mic on throughout.

Music aside, as a believer, getting to read Scripture out loud in that kind of venue means so much. The event takes on almost an entirely different meaning. For me, it's not just a concert; it's also a worship event. And the selections from Luke aren't just words on a page; I believe they're alive as well. The story of Christ is woven into the fiber of my being, and to be able to openly share it with people from all over the world is one of the greatest joys of my life.

In addition to the time for reading Scripture, I get about a minute at the beginning and another 30 seconds or so at the end that are completely unscripted. I can say whatever I want.

Usually I give a benediction. I thank everybody for coming, and I let them know that I've been praying for them the entire time I've been standing up there. And I tell them that God loves each and every one of them; that no matter their walk of life or their faith, they are seen and they are loved. I just put it out there. And Disney keeps inviting me back. How cool is that?

I think I've been a narrator at almost a dozen of the processionals over the years. One year I got to do it on Christmas

Day, which was a thrill. Normally I keep my calendar clear on Christmas Eve and Christmas Day. I've even taken red-eyes from Los Angeles after an evening concert to make sure I was home before my kids came down the stairs Christmas morning. So when Disney asked me to narrate on that Christmas Day, I made it a group decision. I sat the kids down and said, "Okay, we're talking Christmas Eve and Christmas Day. We'll still put up the tree at home, and we can unwrap a few tiny presents at the hotel, but the big stuff is gonna have to wait. Is everyone cool with that?"

"Absolutely!" they said. I think they love the event almost as much as I do. They even helped out with it that year.

There's a little pathway that leads out of the theatre, and every night when I would leave, it would turn into a little ad hoc meet and greet, with people asking for photos and wanting to talk about how much the evening meant to them. Well, the security team started getting nervous, because the line was getting so big that it was becoming a fire hazard. They were going to break it up, but I got together with management and said, "Hey, come on; we gotta figure this out. I'm not turning these people away. It's Christmas."

So we found a little alcove off to the side, away from the main flow of traffic, and moved the party over there. The kids helped orchestrate everything, kept the line moving, and even volunteered to take pictures of entire families. It didn't take long, maybe 30 minutes or so, but I just wasn't willing to let go of the opportunity to meet with people face-to-face and hear their stories.

Actions speak so much louder than words. One of the first songs I learned to play on the guitar when I was little was "They'll Know We Are Christians by Our Love," and I try my best to live that out. As a believer, I have to. If someone walks away after spending time with me and they don't feel genuinely heard, appreciated, and cared for, then I've failed.

But it's bigger than that. It's also the way I live my life in general. All of it is a reflection of my faith. I'm aware that if I constantly complain, exhibit a negative spirit, or tear others down—if all my relationships are in shambles and I'm not loving or serving others—people will look at me and think, *Why would I want to be a part of that?*

I want to live in such a way that people look at me and my family and say, "Gosh, you always seem so happy. No matter what's happening, you've always got smiles on your faces. What's that all about?" And as long as I cling to John 15:5 and remain in God and let Him remain in me, I'll be able to live with joy. Honestly, I can't imagine living any other way. For me, there's simply no way to do life without faith.

Some of my most difficult seasons have come when I wasn't listening for God's leading or when I tried to go it alone. But even then, God was always there, telling me, *Don't worry. I've got you. I'm here, and I'm not going to leave you. This dark season isn't going to last forever. Just stay with Me. I will get you through this.* And He has. Time and time again.

That's the amazing thing about living a life of faith: You're never alone. God is always there. He's always listening, always comforting, always guiding, and always right. Once you surrender the decision-making process to Him, all the pressure falls away. It's not about you anymore—and that is so freeing.

One of the most awesome things about being part of Team Ariel was that I didn't have to do it all. I just had to do my one little part and trust the team to take care of the rest. It was the same with Broadway: I didn't need to worry about the lights or the sets, whether so-and-so was going to make their entrance on time or whether we would sell enough tickets to stay open another week. I just had to do my job and trust everyone else to do theirs. That's all any of us can do—play our part to the best of our ability and trust God to take care of the rest.

The other amazing thing about living a life of faith? No matter how small or insignificant your role might seem, God can use it to accomplish more than you ever imagined. That's what Jesus meant when He said we would "bear much fruit."[2]

When you think about it, my role in *The Little Mermaid* was pretty small—a little bit of back-and-forthing with Scuttle, Flounder, and Sebastian; a quick fight with my dad, King Triton; one song; a quick reprise; then *bam*—silence. But look what God has done with that!

I've been blessed with this "surprise career" for more than three decades now, and sometimes it feels like every day is just more icing on top of an already beautifully decorated cake—just blessing upon blessing, decade after decade. If there are more wonderful surprises to come, great. If not, I'm content. As I told Chris Montan, it's been a great ride.

I really do love my job. In fact, it's not even really a job. It's never been a job. It's a joy, an honor, and a privilege. It's never been about fame or money, awards, or recognition. It's about the faith walk, the journey, and the God-appointments.

It's about all the people whom God, in His great wisdom and mercy, put along my path. All the people I was supposed to learn from, say something to, pray for, or simply sit and be silent with. That's what this journey's been about. And it's still going.

I hope I still have a lot of years of being Ariel ahead of me. But someday if the phone does ring and a voice on the other end brings this extraordinary journey to an end, I hope everyone at Disney and all the people I've encountered and had the privilege of knowing along the way will ultimately know that I loved God, my family, and others, and that I tried to be light and salt and make a positive impact wherever I went and with whomever I met.

From the very beginning, this has been God's journey. I've just been blessed to be a part of it. I hope I've been worthy of the incredible, life-changing ministry He's blessed me with, and that I've made the most of every opportunity He's given me.

It's been an amazing life. It hasn't always been perfect; goodness knows I've made my share of mistakes, and not everything has turned out the way I'd hoped or expected. But I wouldn't trade it for a million anythings, because the good has so outweighed the bad. I'm so very, very grateful—for the good, for the bad, for all of it—and for you.

Thank you so much for being part of my journey and for making it possible for me to do what I love to do. Thank you for loving Ariel, for sharing your stories, and for making an already unbelievable journey even more magical.

Thank you, sweet friend, for letting me be part of your world.

Acknowledgments

My loving God. My Savior, Jesus. Gracious God of second chances: I am nothing apart from You. I surrender all to You. I will forever praise Your name. Thank You for taking my brokenness and making me whole again. Take this little book, with all my big mess, and use it for Your glory and as You desire. Thank You for always loving me.

To the love of my life, my husband, Ray, my very best friend, my constant, my rock: I wouldn't be alive today if it weren't for you. From the moment I met you, I knew we were meant to be together. You saved my life. You never gave up on me . . . even when you should have. Thank you for loving me when I am unlovable. Thank you for believing in me. Thank you for always being my #1 fan and cheerleader. Thank you for blessing me with the two greatest gifts in the world, our children. Thank you for your endless love and loyal commitment to me and our relationship for the past 42 years. I am so blessed to have you as my husband & the amazing dad of our incredible kids. You felt for years that I had a book inside of me to share, and I kept saying a fervent no every time! Thank you so much for being patient with me. I love you with all of my heart, both now and forever.

Looking back over the past four decades, I know beyond a shadow of a doubt that my greatest blessings and most incredible accomplishments are our children. McKinley and Delaney . . . no concert, no job, no show, no recording session, no destination, no experience or added line on a résumé could *ever* begin to compare to the unbelievable privilege of being your mom. I learn so much from both of you every single day, and I want you to know how much I love, respect, and adore you.

McKinley, you have such a beautiful, loving spirit filled with tremendous compassion and unending mercy. You love the underdog and always believe the best about everyone. You don't have a single enemy. Your heart is huge, and you will fight for truth. You have taught me how to love everyone who is different from me, how to be gracious to all, and how to see things from another person's perspective. Your faith is steadfast, and your love for God permeates all you do. You are wise beyond your years, and your work ethic is unparalleled. I so admire your tenacity and your pursuit of excellence. I love how you rise above adversity, forgive so quickly, and deem others more important than yourself. You were, in so many ways, our miracle baby, and I could not love you more. I love you so much, Buddy.

Delaney, you are filled with abundant joy and fervent purpose. You have such a loving, loyal heart and your dad's incredible sense of humor. You are driven, motivated, and such a hard worker. You never give up, no matter the obstacles or challenges you may face. You are steadfast in your love, and you forgive so easily. You have experienced brokenness and have learned how to turn ashes into beauty. I have learned from you how to be inclusive and nonjudgmental and how to let go of anger quickly. Your smile, love for others, and laughter are so very contagious. You have always been so mature emotionally for your age, and you make such great decisions with strong conviction. You listen to the Holy Spirit and are so close to Jesus, and I am so proud and blessed to call you my daughter. I love you so much, my sweet girl.

I treasure my relationships with both of you. I know all the time that our family has spent closely together, our years of homeschooling, and our many travels have bonded us tightly. We are a family built on a firm foundation of love, faith, respect, laughter, and true friendship. To put it simply, we really like each other and enjoy each other's company. I love hanging out with you both. You are so amazing. You are so authentic. You are so genuine. You make me a better person, and I love you both to the moon and back and to the moon again.

Mackenzie, thank you for loving our son with your whole heart. I love you and am thrilled you have joined our family and have become my treasured "daughter in love." You're an incredibly talented photographer, and I'm so honored that you shot my book-cover photo, author photo, and our family photo. Thank you for your countless hours of hard work on this book through concept design and sifting through boxes of photos with me, then scanning and editing. I love your compassionate heart & giving spirit. Your love & kindness are a gift to us all.

Mom, you have loved & supported me my whole life. We've been through so much together, and we have come through with a stronger, more authentic and loving relationship. You are the strongest woman I know, and I love you so much. Thank you for being my mom. Thank you for loving me . . . even though after having a boy and a girl, you really wanted a pony!

My sister, Jill: You've always been by my side since day one. You truly are the kindest, most accepting, most humble person I know. Being in your presence makes me a better person. Your belief in me has carried me for so many years. When I have blown it big-time, you've always been there to pick me up and urge me to move forward. You taught me how to love unconditionally. You have led by example and shown me how to be a loving wife and an encouraging mother, and how to always put family first. I really treasure your wisdom and advice. Thank you for never giving up on me. I am so thankful you are my sister and my best friend. I love you.

Allan, my bro: Although we don't share biological parents, you are my brother and have been since I was 11. Thank you, Bro. You and Kathy have supported and loved me through every stage of my life. I know you're always with me, and I am so very grateful. Thank you for walking through this whole "crazy book journey thing" with me from start to finish. It has been so wonderful to have you—a professional author—reading and editing, helping me every step of the way. You're an amazing guy, and I love you.

Robin and Rhonda, my cousins who have become my dear friends and my adopted sisters, and my sister-in-law, Deb: Thank you for your amazing friendships. I couldn't have made the move to Georgia without knowing you all were here for me and my family. Thank you for your unending love.

My nieces & nephews: I am so thankful for each of you—Ashley, Maureen & Margaret, Paul, Ali & Sasha, as well as all of your wonderful spouses and children. My cousins who chose to call me Aunt Jodi: May May, Kendall, Jenna & Kylie, Ben, Lindsay & Scott, and their families. Love abounds with all of you, and you bring so much overflowing joy to my life.

My lifelong friends, my family: Marcia & Seth, Liz & John, Kathy, Timmy, Lisa & Eric, Gina & Buster—you have all loved me & Ray very well for so many years. Friendships like these are forever. You've loved our kids as your very own. I'm eternally grateful for each of you. I love you all.

My Georgia friends who have become my family: Angela, Allison, Daryl, Lisa, Amie, and Laura, you welcomed me and helped me feel at home with your friendships filled with faith. You point me closer to Jesus.

Thank you to my amazing high school friends, Debbie, Laura, Sam, and Tim . . . your love and support mean the world to me.

Thank you to my brilliant vocal coach, Joan Lader, for keeping my voice strong and healthy and for loving, encouraging, and supporting me for the past 38 years. I love you!

My Disney family: Howard, it all started with you, from my first day of auditions for *Smile* to holding your hand in the hospital and trying to say goodbye. None of the experiences of my life over the past nearly 40 years would have ever happened if I hadn't met you. Thank you for believing in me and trusting me as an artist. Thank you for seeing the best in me when I couldn't. Thank you for taking a huge chance on me. Your brilliance, wisdom, and empathy and your constant, meticulous pursuit of excellence have all made a deep, permanent, lasting imprint upon my heart and my life. Every time I sing our song, I think of you. I honor you and pay tribute to you with every note. I love you, Howard. Thank you for an incredible journey.

Alan, I'm in awe of you. Your talent is so far beyond what I can even begin to comprehend. Your love, kindness, humor, and humility amaze me, and I am honored to work with you. Thank you for the privilege of singing your song every week. I have so much love and respect for you, my friend.

Ron & John, thank you for choosing me to be your Ariel. Your passion, vision, and creativity have changed my life forever. I am so blessed & honored to have been directed by you both. Thank you for the experience of a lifetime.

Roy Disney, thank you for being such a father to me. Your kindness, encouragement, and laughter truly transformed me. I miss you so much.

Michael, Jeffrey, Peter, and the entire cast, crew, and animators of *The Little Mermaid*: Thank you for all the love, care, and talent each of you painstakingly poured into our beautiful, life-changing film. I am forever thankful for all of you.

Glen, thank you for bringing Ariel to life through the talented touch of your pencil. God had a perfect plan in place when He brought us together. Thank you for your friendship and your faith that encourage me. I am so grateful to you and Linda for your love and support in helping me put my life and marriage back together.

Rick, Bryan, Ben, Renee, and my family at Disney Character Voices: I am so thankful for our 33+ years together. We are family, and I am so blessed by your friendship, love, and support. Rick, thank you for being my first friend to read the very first draft of this book, and for all of your help, wisdom, and encouragement. Love to all of you.

Paige, my dear friend of 40+ years and my fellow Disney Classic Princess: I love you, my sweet friend. God has blessed me in huge, beautiful ways because of you being in my life. Thanks so much to you, Linda, and Irene, for our precious friendship and our "Disney Princess Group Text." I am so grateful we can love and support each other always.

Uncle Dana, Les, and Stephanie, thank you so much for being my amazing Disney VIP Tour Guides for all these years, but mostly . . . thank you for being part of our family. We love you all!

Sarah, my publisher: I can't believe you pursued and pursued and pursued me to write this book! What the heck?! Thank you for putting up with my tears, my fears, and everything in between. You knew I didn't want to write a book, but you kept on course with what God was telling you to do. I so admire your patience and tenacity. Thank you for not giving up on me. Thank you for your unending kindness, guidance, encouragement, and wisdom.

To Dean, Andrea, Cassidy, Katie, and the rest of my amazing Tyndale team . . . thank you all for your help and support. I so appreciate all of you!

Carol, my writer: Okay. Holding back tears as I write this. Nope. Can't hold them back . . . lettin' 'em flow. Oh, sweetie . . . yep, I'm calling you sweetie. How many hours did we spend on the phone during the pandemic?! Countless hours and months. So many laughs, but oh, so many tears. Honestly, I wanted to hang up on you so many times! This was the most exhilarating and exhausting experience I have ever been through in my entire life. It was so hard looking back, but you never got angry or impatient with me, even when I was so frustrated at times. You kept building me up and believing in me, even when I walked away from this whole project and canceled the book for a season to really pray and seek God. You kept loving me and pouring kindness over me—*always*. You know this book would not exist without you. Thank you for helping me to be obedient. Thank you for being a brilliant writer. Love you, sweetie.

Thank you so much to all the incredible people who have joined me along the way throughout my journey of life so far. To those from my past, my present, and my future . . . I am so grateful for all of you!

Credits for Chapter Titles

1. **"Maybe He's Right"**

   From Ashman, Howard, lyricist. "Part of Your World." *The Little Mermaid*, music by Alan Menken, copyright © 1988 Walt Disney Music Company (ASCAP)/Wonderland Music Company, Inc. (BMI). All rights reserved. International copyright secured. From the Walt Disney animated feature *The Little Mermaid*, produced by Howard Ashman and John Musker, written and directed by John Musker and Ron Clements.

2. **"I Want More"**

   From Ashman, Howard, lyricist. "Part of Your World." *The Little Mermaid*, music by Alan Menken, copyright © 1988 Walt Disney Music Company (ASCAP)/Wonderland Music Company, Inc. (BMI). All rights reserved. International copyright secured.

3. **"What Good Is Sitting Alone in Your Room?"**

   From Ebb, Fred, lyricist. "Cabaret." *Cabaret*, music by John Kander, Alley Music and Trio Music, 1967.

4. **"What I Want from You Is . . . Your Voice"**

   From Ashman, Howard, lyricist. "Poor Unfortunate Souls." *The Little Mermaid*, music by Alan Menken, copyright © 1988 Walt Disney Music Company (ASCAP)/Wonderland Music Company, Inc. (BMI). All rights reserved. International copyright secured.

5. *"I Saw You and the World Went Away"*
   From Sondheim, Stephen, lyricist. "Tonight." *West Side Story*,
   music by Leonard Bernstein, copyright © 1956, 1957 Amberson
   Holdings LLC and Stephen Sondheim. Copyright renewed.

6. *"Sick of Swimmin', Ready to Stand"*
   From Ashman, Howard, lyricist. "Part of Your World." *The
   Little Mermaid*, music by Alan Menken, copyright © 1988
   Walt Disney Music Company (ASCAP)/Wonderland Music
   Company, Inc. (BMI). All rights reserved. International
   copyright secured.

7. *"Ask 'Em My Questions and Get Some Answers"*
   From Ashman, Howard, lyricist. "Part of Your World." *The Little
   Mermaid*, music by Alan Menken, copyright © 1988 Walt Disney
   Music Company (ASCAP)/Wonderland Music Company, Inc.
   (BMI). All rights reserved. International copyright secured.

8. *"Life's Full of Tough Choices, Isn't It?"*
   From Ashman, Howard, lyricist. "Poor Unfortunate Souls." *The
   Little Mermaid*, music by Alan Menken, copyright © 1988 Walt
   Disney Music Company (ASCAP)/Wonderland Music Company,
   Inc. (BMI). All rights reserved. International copyright secured.

9. *"When's It My Turn?"*
   From Ashman, Howard, lyricist. "Part of Your World." *The Little
   Mermaid*, music by Alan Menken, copyright © 1988 Walt Disney
   Music Company (ASCAP)/Wonderland Music Company, Inc.
   (BMI). All rights reserved. International copyright secured.

10. *"Poor Unfortunate Soul"*
    From Ashman, Howard, lyricist. "Poor Unfortunate Souls." *The
    Little Mermaid*, music by Alan Menken, copyright © 1988 Walt
    Disney Music Company (ASCAP)/Wonderland Music Company,
    Inc. (BMI). All rights reserved. International copyright secured.

11. *"No Time Will Be Better"*
    From Ashman, Howard, lyricist. "Kiss the Girl." *The Little
    Mermaid*, music by Alan Menken, copyright © 1988 Walt Disney
    Music Company (ASCAP)/Wonderland Music Company, Inc.
    (BMI). All rights reserved. International copyright secured.

12. *"If You Keep On Believing"*
    From Livingston, Jerry, lyricist. "A Dream Is a Wish Your Heart
    Makes." *Cinderella*, music by Mack David, Al Hoffman, and Jerry
    Livingston, Walt Disney Music, 1948.

13. *"Strollin' Along down the . . . What's That Word Again?"*
    From Ashman, Howard, lyricist. "Part of Your World." *The Little
    Mermaid*, music by Alan Menken, copyright © 1988 Walt Disney
    Music Company (ASCAP)/Wonderland Music Company, Inc.
    (BMI). All rights reserved. International copyright secured.

14. *"Don't Underestimate the Importance of Body Language"*
    From Ashman, Howard, lyricist. "Poor Unfortunate Souls." *The
    Little Mermaid*, music by Alan Menken, copyright © 1988 Walt
    Disney Music Company (ASCAP)/Wonderland Music Company,
    Inc. (BMI). All rights reserved. International copyright secured.

15. *"Wouldn't You Think I'm the Girl, the Girl Who Has
    Ev'rything?"*
    From Ashman, Howard, lyricist. "Part of Your World." *The Little
    Mermaid*, music by Alan Menken, copyright © 1988 Walt Disney
    Music Company (ASCAP)/Wonderland Music Company, Inc.
    (BMI). All rights reserved. International copyright secured.

16. *"What Would I Pay to Stay Here beside You?"*
    From Ashman, Howard, lyricist. "Part of Your World (Reprise)." *The
    Little Mermaid*, music by Alan Menken, copyright © 1988 Walt
    Disney Music Company (ASCAP)/Wonderland Music Company,
    Inc. (BMI). All rights reserved. International copyright secured.

17. **"Who Could Ask for Anything More?"**
    From Gershwin, George and Ira Gershwin. "I Got Rhythm." *Crazy for You*, performed at Shubert Theatre in 1992, New World Music, 1930.

18. **"But Not for Me"**
    From Gershwin, George and Ira Gershwin. "But Not for Me." *Crazy for You*, performed at Shubert Theatre in 1992, New World Music, 1930.

19. **"Someone to Watch Over Me"**
    From Gershwin, George and Ira Gershwin. "Someone to Watch Over Me." *Crazy for You*, performed at Shubert Theatre in 1992, WB Music, 1926.

20. **"Authority Should Derive from the Consent of the Governed, Not from the Threat of Force!"**
    From Unkrich, Lee, dir. *Toy Story 3*. Walt Disney Pictures and Pixar Animation Studios, 2010.

21. **"I Don't Know When, I Don't Know How"**
    From Ashman, Howard, lyricist. "Part of Your World (Reprise)." *The Little Mermaid*, music by Alan Menken, copyright © 1988 Walt Disney Music Company (ASCAP)/Wonderland Music Company, Inc. (BMI). All rights reserved. International copyright secured.

22. **"Just beyond the Meadows of Joy and the Valley of Contentment"**
    From Lima, Kevin, dir. *Enchanted*. 2007; Walt Disney Pictures, 2007.

23. **"My One and Only"**
    From Gershwin, George and Ira Gershwin. "My One and Only." *My One and Only*, performed at St. James Theatre in 1983, WB Music, 1927.

Notes

2: "I WANT MORE"

1. "Wouldn't It Be Loverly?" copyright © 1956 by Alan Jay Lerner and Frederick Loewe. All rights administered by Chappell & Co., Inc.

3: "WHAT GOOD IS SITTING ALONE IN YOUR ROOM?"

1. "Cabaret," songwriters John Kander/Fred Ebb/Jean-claude Cosson, lyrics copyright © Trio Music Company, Alley Music Corp., Times Square Music Publications Company, Trio Music Company Inc., Trio Music Co., Inc.
2. Matthew 5:15.

4: "WHAT I WANT FROM YOU IS . . . YOUR VOICE"

1. "For Good," music and lyrics by Stephen Schwartz, 2003, lyrics copyright © Greydog Music.
2. Isaiah 41:10.

5: "I SAW YOU AND THE WORLD WENT AWAY"

1. "Tonight," from *West Side Story*, music by Leonard Bernstein and lyrics by Stephen Sondheim, copyright © 1956, 1957 Amberson Holdings LLC and Stephen Sondheim. Copyright renewed. Leonard Bernstein Music Publishing Company LLC, Publisher.

10: "POOR UNFORTUNATE SOUL"

1. Matthew 7:12, MSG.

11: "NO TIME WILL BE BETTER"

1. "Disneyland," lyrics by Howard Ashman, copyright ©1986 by Chappell & Co., Famous Music Corporation, Red Bullet Music, and Shop Talk Ltd.
2. See Matthew 5:13-14, MSG.

13: "STROLLIN' ALONG DOWN THE . . . WHAT'S THAT WORD AGAIN?"

1. Isaiah 30:21, NIV.

19: "SOMEONE TO WATCH OVER ME"

1. Philippians 4:6-7.

20: "AUTHORITY SHOULD DERIVE FROM THE CONSENT OF THE GOVERNED, NOT FROM THE THREAT OF FORCE!"

1. Quoted in Bruce Orwall, "Many Toy Stores Decide to Give Buzz Lightyear a Second Chance," *Wall Street Journal*, November 26, 1999, https://www.wsj.com/articles/SB943574124360705967.

23: "MY ONE AND ONLY"

1. Matthew 6:21, NIV.

24: JOHN 15:5

1. NIV.
2. John 15:8, NIV.

About the Authors

JODI BENSON is best known around the world as the beloved voice of Ariel in the Academy Award–winning Disney animated feature film *The Little Mermaid*. Jodi also created the voice of Barbie in Disney/Pixar's *Toy Story 2* and *Toy Story 3* and delighted Disney fans with a cameo in *Enchanted* before reprising her role as Ariel in *Ralph Breaks the Internet*. In 2011, Disney honored Jodi's contributions by making her a Disney Legend. An accomplished singer, dancer, and actress, Jodi made her starring-role debut on Broadway performing the iconic song "Disneyland" in the Howard Ashman/Marvin Hamlisch musical *Smile*, and she earned a Tony nomination for her role as Polly Baker in the hit Gershwin musical *Crazy for You*. Still entertaining audiences across the country and around the world, Jodi is currently living in North Georgia with her wonderful husband, Ray. They enjoy spending time with their two amazing adult children, McKinley and Delaney.

CAROL TRAVER has been helping authors shape their stories for more than a decade. Her collaborative efforts include *With My Eyes Wide Open* by KoRn guitarist Brian "Head"

Welch and *I'm No Angel* by former Victoria's Secret runway model Kylie Bisutti. As a developmental editor and writing collaborator, Carol has created and contributed to the development of countless other memoirs, as well as many other Christian living, self-help, and devotional books. She lives in the Chicago area.